It's the Thought that Counts

The Power of Thought, Feeling, and Faith

David Hamilton ☺

It's the Thought that Counts

The Power of Thought, Feeling, and Faith

By Dr David R. Hamilton Ph.D.

H
Hamilton

A catalogue record for this title is available from the British Library

ISBN 0 9550005 0 5

Printed and bound in the UK by Antony Rowe Ltd, Bumpers Farm Industrial Estate, Chippenham, Wilts.

Dr David R. Hamilton
62 Viewfield Road
Banknock, Bonnybridge
Scotland, FK4 1TG

About the author

David Hamilton gained a first class honours degree in biological and medicinal chemistry and a Ph.D. in organic chemistry before going on to be a scientist in the pharmaceutical industry in 1995. After four years he left and has since worked as a motivational speaker, co-founded an international relief charity, co-organised a 9-day, 24-event festival of peace called Spirit Aid, and worked as a college lecturer in both chemistry and ecology. He has been featured on TV, BBC radio, and has been the subject of national newspaper articles. He spends most of his time writing, giving talks and leading workshops on the topics of his writing.

Acknowledgements

I consider myself to be truly blessed in being surrounded by so many kind, patient, understanding, and generous people.

I would like to thank my life partner Elizabeth Caproni. Her never-ending love and support has been an inspiration to me and has often lifted me and guided me along my current path. Without her, this book would never have gained its present form.

I would also like to thank my parents, Janette and Robert Hamilton, who brought me into this world, loved me and supported me throughout every endeavour of my life, and who taught me from an early age that "It's the Thought That Counts."

I would also like to thank Elma and Peter Caproni who made me a part of their family, loving me and supporting me through numerous challenging times.

To my many friends, past and present, who have helped guide me on my spiritual path I am also grateful. In particular I will always remember the journey of Spirit Aid and all who participated in it.

A great big Thank You to all who patiently read this book and offered me some feedback: Margaret McCathie, Kenny McCathie, June Moore, Siobhan Moore, Dave Clarkson, Olivia Barham, Ann Brocklebank, Stan Giles, Liz Ivory, Bryce Redford, Joyce Bunton, Kenny McDougall, Seth Gardiner, and Andrea Lomas. I would also like to thank Thom Hartmann for endorsing the book.

For helpful answers to some of my questions regarding chapter 3, I would like to thank Professor Eric Kandel, year 2000 Nobel Laureate for Medicine or Physiology. I would also like to thank Dr

Ernest Rossi for helpful answers and for taking the time and effort to send me some important scientific publications on psychosocial genomics that helped evolve chapter 3 into its present form. This help was given having never seen the book.

I would also like to thank Glasgow University Library, The Homeopathic Hospital in Glasgow, and Paul Stevens in the Koestler Parapsychology Unit of Edinburgh University for helping me obtain valuable scientific information for the book.

To all the scientists who have painstakingly done the research that I have reported in this book, you have helped many people to recognise that what they always believed just might be true, really is.

To the writers of the many mind-body-spirit books I have read since leaving the pharmaceutical industry in 1999, you have inspired me in many ways.

Contents

Preface

This book was written so that people could realise that what they always thought just might be true, really is. I have used science to make a clear and credible picture. I have attempted to explain the science in the simplest terms possible to make it accessible to more people. To that end, it can be read by people with no background in science and has been tested on such individuals for ease of understanding of the concepts.

Most of the science has been published in scientific journals and I merely extracted the relevant portions and repackaged the words to make the outcome of the research accessible to the ordinary reader who is unfamiliar with scientific jargon.

I have made a few extrapolations of the conclusions of some research, fusing with my own ideas gained from having a very broad view of the fields of mind-body science, spirituality, and consciousness.

Some of the research quoted has not been published in peer reviewed scientific journals. However this does not mean that it is not valid. There are often a number of reasons for such situations. For instance, I have personally conducted experiments but have not gathered enough data – mainly due to time constraints – to publish. But this does not mean that the research is invalid. It just means that the results *may* not be as reliable. Some aspects of it might not be as accurate as they could be but I do believe that they point towards a real phenomenon. I believe that we are on the brink of a major breakthrough in our understanding of consciousness and the constant interplay between mind and matter.

Some of the research I have discussed might sound 'way out there' - like Digital Biology discussed in chapter 5 for instance. I think the research conducted by the late Jacques Benveniste is highly exciting and deserved to be mentioned. I do believe that time will reveal the research to be the foundation of a new approach to medicine. If not, then it's all part of the path of scientific discovery.

To the average academic scientist, some of what is discussed in this book might fall into this category. I make no apologies for this. As history has shown us, the path of scientific discovery frequently uncovers what first appears to be ridiculous, only later for our understanding of the way things work to be modified to embrace the new ideas.

The second half of the book brings spirituality into play. There is less science in this part and more use of intuition as I present a view of the world that is probably beyond scientific proof and can only be grasped by personal experience. But this is still science, only a different kind of science that is personal to the individual, making everyone a scientist in his or her own life.

I introduce God, who is a daily friend in my life, and suggest that 'we are all Gods' simply suffering from a little amnesia. I also present my intuitive belief that we collectively create our world, while touching upon some theories of quantum physics that have parallels with eastern mystical thought to back it up. In chapter 12, Higher Self condensation of DNA is a personal theory of mine that feels right to me, and time may or may not ever find a way to prove or disprove this. I invite the reader to 'feel' if it makes sense to them.

I end the book in the way I like to end all of my talks – helping the reader to recognise the love, kindness, and compassion everywhere around them. When we choose to love, be kind, and exercise compassion in our personal lives, everything changes. Everything. Go on, try it out! Let us, then, begin our journey of change.

Dr David R. Hamilton Ph.D.
February 2005

Disclaimer
Throughout this book, the author is not offering medical advice of any kind. Readers with any medical conditions are advised to seek advice from a qualified physician.

It's the Thought that Counts

The Power of Thought, Feeling, and Faith

Introduction

The book is about the effects of thoughts, feelings, and faith. The first half describes the effects on the human body and the second half describes their effects on our personal lives and the world. Although much of the book is backed up with science, it is written in a simple, easy to read, style that is accessible to anyone.

The book starts with a simple introduction to the way our thoughts and feelings affect our bodies. For instance, how a thought of something that embarrasses you might turn your face red. Similarly, stressful thinking about, say, being late for an appointment alters the rhythms of your heart, depresses your immune system, and can lead to a number of serious illnesses. It is not the being late, but the thoughts *about* being late that causes the disharmony.

This leads onto how belief can cure. The book gives some examples of the placebo effect and how it cures between 10-100% of people in medical trials, depending upon the type of illness and the nature of the trial. Science now understands the placebo effect as movements of the 'molecules of emotion' known as neuropeptides. When a person receives a placebo and they believe it is a real medicine they usually recover. This is because a belief is a feeling of certainty. The feeling produces neuropeptides in the brain that travel to the site of disease and switch on the body's own natural healing capacity.

The next chapter discusses how thoughts and feelings even affect our DNA. One of the most powerful scientific examples cited in this chapter is the effect of a mother's loving touch on her infant.

Studies have shown that genes that determine the amount of growth hormones in the infant's body are switched on by a mother's loving touch but are temporarily switched off when such love is deprived. Abused or neglected children deprived of love in this way are often found to have abnormally small amounts of growth hormones.

Contrary to what we've previously believed, that a person is stuck with whichever genes they inherited, the science of psychosocial genomics has shown that our thoughts and feelings can actually switch genes on and off. Therefore anyone has the ability to be whatever they choose, should they want it enough and believe that it is possible.

Chapter 4 outlines some of the science behind 'healing by touch', giving compelling results of the effects of healing touch on humans, animals, plants, and on isolated organisms like bacteria and enzymes held in a jar.

The next chapter is called 'Good Vibrations' and discusses how thoughts and feelings are actually vibrations that imprint whatever they come into contact with. It discusses some of the research that shows how emotions affect water, mentioning Masaru Emoto's work with crystal structures of water and also that of Professor William Tiller at Stanford University, where he used scientific instruments to see changes in the molecular structure of water molecules. The chapter also describes Digital Biology - the work of the late Jacques Benveniste – where biological organisms respond to vibrations just as good as they respond to chemicals.

The next chapter discusses distant healing and prayer, outlining compelling scientific research showing that intentions travel great distances and have powerful biological effects. In one particular example, two groups of people were kept 25 metres apart in separate rooms, one group being the 'influencers' and the other being the 'receivers'. The receivers were hooked up to scientific measuring devices that recorded fluctuations in their skin resistance. These studies showed that the skin resistance of the receivers changed at the instant the influencers thought about them.

The chapter also gives some studies that have been published in peer reviewed mainstream scientific journals, proving the power of prayer. For instance a 1988 report in the Southern Medical Journal describes how the people prayed for, out of a group of 393 patients who underwent heart surgery, recovered almost twice as fast as the people not prayed for.

Chapter 7 begins part two of the book and is titled, 'The Nature of Reality'. In simple to understand terms it describes the interconnectedness of all things, drawing clear parallels between eastern and western thought. It describes how consciousness is the fundamental building block of all matter and how all things condense out of the 'field'. The condensation process is analogous to the way that steam condenses to form water. All things, then, are connected and are susceptible to human thought and emotion. The chapter also discusses our connection through the collective unconscious and how we are collectively evolving, pointing out examples in the world where the power of love and the human spirit is more obvious than ever before.

The next chapter backs this up with experimental evidence that has measured group consciousness. The chapter also describes how it is possible for us to make significant positive changes in the world if many of us come together with a common purpose. It cites examples of mass prayer organised by James Twyman, Gregg Braden, and Doreen Virtue, that had a global effect and also suggests how we could use the media to send out positive messages.

Chapter 9 discusses the nature of the human spirit and how the Higher Self purposely creates each person exactly as they are. It also shows how we *are* the Higher Self, simply experiencing a little amnesia. It explains that we are on a journey of experiences, each offering us a unique opportunity to recognise that we are 'in this world but not of this world'. It explains that our temporary state of amnesia is why we appear to lack the abilities to heal ourselves of any illness or to make positive changes in our lives. It is a cosmic placebo effect. In the words of chapter 9:

"Our deep belief in who we think we are causes us to perform in accordance with what limits we believe in. But we do not lack any of these abilities. They are latent within us, just as the real power of an iceberg lies beneath the surface." The chapter suggests that such abilities are 'encoded' in our DNA as sets of genes.

"Our beliefs affect whether such genes are on or off in the same way that a belief in athletic ability, for instance, will usually make a person a better athlete. At present, these 'healing' or 'transformational' genes are switched off in most people. But it is likely that such genes merely await our genuine recognition of who we really are."

The next chapter is a short chapter pulling together and contrasting the different effects of love and fear on human biology that have been mentioned in previous chapters. The purpose of this chapter is to reinforce the healing power of love by showing clear scientific evidence in support of it. Like the study of rabbits fed a high fat diet and monitored for atherosclerosis. During the study, one group of the rabbits had been removed from their cages every day and lovingly stroked by a technician, unknown to the scientists. When the results of the study came in it showed that there was 60% less atherosclerosis in this group.

Chapter 11 is called 'Mass reality' and describes how we collectively create world events. Just as a person unconsciously condenses every particle that forms their body, we collectively condense everything we see around us. The chapter draws upon scientific evidence from previous chapters to explain this, but more importantly highlights how we can change it by changing ourselves.

Chapter 12 is perhaps the most radical in that it describes how the higher self condenses each person's DNA so that they develop in the way chosen before birth. It explains how the intention of the higher self, deep in each person's unconscious, is the blueprint that is responsible for the condensed genetic structure of each person's DNA.

Reminding the reader of the fact that thoughts and emotions switch genes on and off, this blueprint also serves as the deep psychological trigger that switches on specific genes throughout their life. I suggest that these thought vibrations of the Higher Self are responsible for the rhythmic and wavelike manner in which genes switch on and off, drawing upon very recent evidence from genetics that shows how the human body grows through temporal waves of genes switching on, like in the construction of the central nervous system in a foetus.

The chapter also describes how we have a collectively conscious effect on our genetic evolution. Our collective level of consciousness influences the condensation of our genetic blueprint in succeeding generations.

The next chapter is another short one, reinforcing the point that we create the world the way it is and emphasising the importance of each individual in the world, regardless of race, religion, background, or status. That every person is special and important! It encourages us to take personal responsibility for our own lives and for the world by encouraging us to look at how we behave, honestly, because what we project outwards, through our thoughts, words, feelings, and actions mix with everyone else's and help paint the landscape of events in the world. It reinforces the point that things only change when we change.

The final chapter is called, "Three Simple Rules." These rules are Love for Self, Love for Others, and Love for Nature. It is suggested that living by these simple rules can not only transform a person's life, but can have a miraculous effect on everyone around them and on the world.

1

Mind and Body

The body and mind are intertwined. Every thought, feeling, and intention sends ripples throughout your body. The results depend upon the nature of your thoughts, feelings, and intentions. They can be so powerful that they even affect your genetic code.

It is so entangled with the mind that our genes are actually coloured by how we think and feel on a daily basis. Having a particular gene that might produce a disease, or protect you from disease, for example, can be switched on and off according to how you process the daily experiences of your life.

The implications of this are enormous. Every function of the human body is susceptible to thoughts and feelings. Scientific studies on DNA have even shown that infants require a mother's loving touch for growth. When this touch is consistently deprived, some of the genes that are responsible for growth simply switch off.

The entire body is hardwired to physically feel every emotion. And as it does so, our emotional challenges occasionally show up as physical symptoms in our bodies. Although there are many different causes of cancer, for instance, one factor is the suppression of negative emotion. It has been shown that cancers generally progress fastest in people who hold in deep emotional pain, often gathered over many years. The great news is that releasing the pain can halt and even reverse the cancer.

We regularly cure aches, pains, illnesses, and diseases using our minds, although most of the time we are unaware of what we did. Science has proven that a person who believes he or she is receiving a medicine, although it is really a dummy one – a placebo – will usually be cured because of their belief. For instance, in one scientific study patients were given morphine for a serious pain every day for 3 days, but on the fourth day the morphine was secretly swapped for a placebo – a saltwater solution. Yet the patients received pain relief as they did before, and even the medical tests recorded the same physiological changes that they recorded when the patient received morphine. They believed that they were receiving morphine, and why wouldn't they? The belief simply neutralised the pain.

Placebo effects like these rely on blind faith, where the patient is not aware that they are receiving a placebo, but everyone can learn to harness the power of their thoughts and feelings to bring about positive health effects in their own body. Visualisation techniques, for instance, are regularly used by thousands of people and have often produced what may be seen as nothing short of miracles.

And we can even heal each other. The numerous methods of healing by touch are used by a growing number of people all over the world. In fact, a 1998 study estimated that over 40,000 nurses in the USA practised such therapies. That number is much greater now. In the UK, a year 2000 estimate suggested that there were around three times more practitioners of Reiki than there were doctors and nurses.

There is a large volume of research to back up these therapies, much of it done under strict scientifically controlled conditions. Some of these studies even show that people can mentally influence the growth rate of biological organisms held in test tubes. Amazing, but true!

Studies have also shown why it is that many people can be aware when someone is staring at them. Researchers have found that people sitting in one room were responding to thoughts about them from people in another room 25 metres away. While hooked up to scientific instruments their skin would show minor changes in electrical resistance depending upon the type of thought held about them.

All of these studies, and many more, will be discussed later in the book. So too will be the fact that according to our thoughts, feelings, and our beliefs we create the experiences of our lives. And the good news is that we can change any aspect of our lives simply by changing our attitudes.

Collectively we also create events in the world. As well as showing that the body and mind are connected, science has also learned that we are intimately connected to each other. Everyone and everything share a bond such that every thought and feeling sends ripples throughout the entire universe. While each person has what may be called a 'mental and emotional climate', representing his or her general mental and emotional state, we share a collective mental and emotional climate. And just as our personal climates influence what happens to us in our personal lives, our collective climate influences what happens to us on a world scale. What goes on all over the world is merely a projection of how we collectively, think and feel.

But before we get ahead of ourselves, let us first explore some of the obvious ways in which the body and mind are connected.

Have you ever realised that when you cry it is your thoughts and feelings that cause your body to produce tears? Thoughts and feelings of happiness or sadness set in motion a series of internal events in your body that climax in a deluge of tears. Mind affecting biology!

An embarrassing thought might turn your face red. A pleasant thought, on the other hand, can alter the rhythms of your heart and even raise the strength of your immune system. For both these to happen, a thought must have affected your biology.

Sexual arousal is also a mind-body phenomenon. Imagination can cause hormonal changes in women and physically obvious changes in men. In these very common ways, thoughts and emotions influence your biology.

On the health front you are probably well aware that stressful thinking can cause a whole range of illnesses, and this has been well documented in the scientific literature. For example, scientific studies have shown that mental and emotional stress can cause heart disease.

Have you ever imagined dire consequences of not getting something done on time, or even stressed yourself out at the thought of being late for an appointment? This sort of stress can eventually bring about internal bodily changes that lead to heart disease. But ultimately, the events did not cause the disease, the mental processes did. It wasn't your being late; it was your thoughts *about* being late.

The health effects of how we think and feel are extremely far reaching. Most medical professionals will agree that the state of mind of many patients admitted to their surgeries is indeed responsible for their illness.

What is less well known, but also true, is the reverse: that your biology can affect your thoughts and emotions. This is pretty obvious if you think about it.

For example, when a woman has her period there are hormonal changes in her body that cause her emotional ups and downs, which affect her thinking. Changes in her biology have brought about changes in her thoughts and emotions.

Furthermore, chemical changes in the brain can make a person feel emotionally high or low. For example, opiate drugs like heroin and morphine can alter emotion. And endorphins, which are the body's own natural opiates, do a similar job.

So mind-body communication goes both ways. Mind to body and body to mind, and it is so smooth that many scientists, just as they refer to space and time as space-time, now refer to the body and mind as the same thing – the bodymind. One cannot be disentangled from the other.

A lot of modern research has gone into this. For instance, the Institute of Heartmath published a scientific study in 1995, in the 'American Journal of Cardiology', which showed the effects of some forms of positive or negative thinking on the heart. They found that thoughts of appreciation (positive) or anger (negative) produced opposite effects in the body.

In the study, a group of twelve people were asked to think 'appreciation' and another twelve were asked to think 'anger'. Meanwhile scientists monitored their hearts.

After performing computer analysis on the heartbeats, the scientists discovered that the hearts of the people thinking 'appreciation' had been beating more smoothly and regularly - called 'internal coherence' - than the hearts of the people who were thinking 'anger'. And this type of coherence has a knock-on effect in the rest of your body.

It is well known that something that is vibrating coherently can 'entrain' neighbouring things to the same smooth rhythm. For example if you were to swing a large pendulum and lots of smaller pendulums at different rates in a room, then leave and come back later, the smaller pendulums would be swinging with the same rhythm as the large one.

The large pendulum entrains, or 'inspires', the smaller pendulums. Similarly, if you hit a tuning fork it will inspire other nearby tuning forks to vibrate at the same speed.

Internal coherence in the heart entrains other organs into a similar coherent and healthy state. In a sense positive thinking can cause all of the organs to sing to the same tune, bringing balance and harmony to your body. You have probably noticed in your personal life that when you feel consistently positive, people sing to the same tune as you and your whole life develops a degree of balance and harmony. The same thing happens in your body.

In a 1995 publication, the Institute of Heartmath also showed that positive and negative thinking could affect the body's immune system. They monitored the amounts of salivary immunoglobulin A (s-IgA) after each person in the study thought 'care and compassion' (positive) or 'anger and frustration' (negative).

Salivary immunoglobulin A is a part of the immune system found in the saliva that can neutralise bacteria that enters your mouth, from your food for example. A large amount of it indicates a strong immune system whereas a small amount indicates a weakened system.

The Heartmath scientists found that 'care and compassion' produced a stronger immune system than 'anger and frustration'.

In fact, they found that just five minutes of 'care and compassion' caused the immune system to be elevated for five hours, while five minutes of 'anger and frustration' depressed it for five hours.

So just like a teacher might say that a person could create positive life experiences by thinking positive, a person can also create positive states of health by doing the same thing. In other words health, just like life, can become positive or negative by the way that we choose to think.

Some people use daily affirmations to keep their minds positive. There is a well known affirmation, created by French psychotherapist Emile Coué, that reads, "*Every day in every way I am getting better and better.*"

Another route to generating a positive attitude is laughter, which is also mind – body communication. When you hear a funny joke or see something funny it is the mental associations you make that produces the laughter, causing your 'side-splitting' movements.

And the physical shaking, coupled with the huge grin on your face, is the last thing to happen. A lot more goes on beneath the surface, all initiated by your mental pictures.

For instance, laughter increases oxygen levels in the blood. It also produces endorphins (feel-good hormones), which explains why it makes you feel so good. It also affects the entire hormone (endocrine) system. Scientific studies have even shown that it strengthens the immune system and therefore helps the body to keep disease away.

If you are remembering a time when you laughed heartily then your body will probably be undergoing these kinds of changes right now. You might even be able to feel them.

So we know that looking at life light heartedly and positively can create good health, but it is not always easy to be so consistently positive.

With the exception of Homer Simpson and a few meditation masters, most people's minds are chaotic, constantly jumping back and forth between topics and initiating a range of moods. The body mirrors the mind. A chaotic mind inspires chaotic biology.

Changing this nature is one of the goals of meditation. As the mind becomes peaceful during meditation, the body's functions become more coherent and so the body becomes healthier. Consistent meditation helps retain this state in daily life.

It has been the subject of a great deal of scientific study, particularly since the arrival of Indian Yogi, Paramahansa Yogananda, in the USA in 1920. He described spiritual masters, whom he called "saints," that lived to great ages, rarely contracted illness, and who could perform great feats. Among other things they practised kriya yoga, which is a form of meditation based upon scientific principles.

Since that time several hundred scientific studies have been conducted on meditation and how it affects health, some of them pointing to why these saints could defy the normal aging process.

One of the main reasons our bodies wear out as we age is because of a gradual deterioration of the endocrine system, which is the hormonal engine in the body. A drop in the levels of some important hormones accompanies this deterioration.

For instance, levels of 'Human Growth Hormone', which helps to keep us healthy and repair our bodies, and the hormone DHEA (dehydroepiandrosterone), which helps to minimise stress, improve memory, and protect the brain from damage, usually drop as we age.

And one of the main factors affecting the deterioration of the endocrine system is the wear and tear brought about by mental and emotional stress. So stress speeds up aging. You have probably heard stories of people under extreme stress whose hair turned white almost overnight.

Meditation is often used as an antidote to stress and has been found to increase DHEA levels. In fact, in a meditation study, a group of forty five year old males who regularly meditated were found to have twenty three percent more DHEA than a similar group who didn't meditate. In women, the meditators had forty seven percent more DHEA.

And another scientific study found that for every twenty percent increase in DHEA there was a forty eight percent drop in heart disease and a thirty six percent drop in death from any cause.

A study into transcendental meditation, which is a form of meditation that uses mantras, even found that people who practiced it for more than five years were physiologically twelve years younger than their chronological age. Could it be that meditation is better than botox?

Some forms of meditation use visualisation, although visualisation alone can be used to have a direct affect on the health of the body. It can be thought of as 'thinking in pictures'. If your thoughts affect the body then so must pictures that you visualise.

In the book "*Creating Miracles*", by Carolyn Miller MD, there is a story of a man who used a visualisation technique that he learned from Shakti Gawain's bestselling book, "*Creative Visualisation.*"

Once fit and active, he had suffered liver damage through an illness. After many weeks in hospital he was told that his liver was so badly damaged that he would have to spend the rest of his life with tubes going in and out of his body.

After reading about creative visualisation he decided to visualise having a healthy liver in his body. Over the next few months he spent many hours visualising a process of cleaning his liver, one cell at a time, with an imaginary toothbrush. At first he pictured it as a black blob but using his imaginary toothbrush he slowly began to clean it and picture it turning a healthy pink colour.

After a few months he had an accident in his home and one of the tubes was torn out of his body. He was rushed to hospital where the doctors prepared him for an operation.

But when he was x-rayed, the surgeon was astonished to discover that his liver had completely regenerated and was in perfect condition. There are many similar stories of the power of visualisation.

As we know, thoughts can also create disease. Most people who get sick are not even aware of the active role they might have played in the process. If everybody was to suddenly know how their thoughts and emotions could create and cure disease then there would be a lot of people changing what they focus upon.

Stress is a common example of the role of the mind in disease, but the mind can have an active role in the creation of even the most serious of diseases.

One of the major accelerators of cancer, for example, is suppressed negative emotion. Over the course of a number of years a person might hold in lots of negative thoughts and feelings, like emotional pain, anxiety, anger, frustration, or resentment.

While some people have an emotional release valve where they speak to someone about their issues and their pain, beat a pillow, or even shout and curse, others store it all up inside. But research has shown that there is a relationship between the growth of emotional pain and a tumour growing inside the body when a person has cancer. Please note, however, that this does not mean that suppressed negative emotion *causes* cancer, only that it may speed it up if a person *has* cancer.

In 1989 James Gross, of the University of California at Berkeley, actually published a summary of eighteen individual scientific studies that had been conducted and reported in the scientific journals over the previous thirty or so years, that showed a clear link between suppressing negative emotions and the progression of the cancer in cancer patients.

One of the earliest of these studies dates back to 1954 when researchers studied the personality types of fifty patients and showed how they could be related to the development of various cancers.

It was clear that cancers progressed fastest in people who had high levels of anxiety but held it in, pretending that everything was fine in their lives, instead of showing it or discharging it.

The correlation was so clear in this particular study that the scientists were able to accurately predict the rate at which cancer would progress, in seventy eight percent of people, simply according to their personality type.

A similar study in 1985 described an obvious relationship between the thickness of tumours and what is known as 'Nonverbal Type C Personality'.

Tumours were thickest in Type C people, who were described as being 'cooperative, unassertive, and suppressing negative emotion'.

A similar relationship was found between HIV and suppressed emotion. In 1996, scientists at UCLA reported their findings in the journal, 'Psychosomatic Medicine'. They showed that HIV progressed at a rate that depended upon the degree to which gay men came 'out of the closet'.

The scientists studied eighty HIV positive gay men and discovered that it progressed slowest in those who were open about the sexuality.

For example they found that men who were most 'in the closet' reached a critically low immune count forty percent faster, developed AIDS thirty eight percent quicker, and average mortality was reached twenty one percent faster.

It may seem difficult to take something positive from what seems to be the case that suppressing negative emotion can be dangerous to health, but as well as showing us the relationship these studies also imply that releasing the pain could slow down and even cure serious diseases.

In fact, in 1988 Pennebaker, Kiecolt-Glaser, and Glaser published a scientific paper that described a link between the immune system and releasing built-up emotion.

When the patients wrote about past thoughts and traumas, and thoroughly resolved their feelings about them, their immune systems got stronger.

The following year a research team published their findings in the medical journal 'The Lancet' where they showed that expressing emotion even prolonged the life of cancer patients.

Their research involved eighty-six women with metastatic breast cancer who were invited to participate in therapy where they were able to express stored up emotions while being emotionally supported throughout the process.

The scientists reported that the women who underwent this therapy lived almost twice as long as women in the same study who didn't.

And in her life-changing book, "The Journey", Brandon Bays described curing herself of a 'basketball sized' tumour in her abdomen, in six weeks, principally through releasing suppressed negative emotion.

She described the process as being like peeling off the layers of emotion as if peeling an onion. In a demonstration of the link between mind and body, layers of her tumour peeled off too.

Of course, not everyone who suppresses negative emotion will get ill. These studies reflect a set of scientific experiments that homed in on a particular area, which is often the case in science. There are a large number of competing factors that can cause cancers and accelerate the course of any disease.

Also, even though there is an obvious link between emotion and the immune system, this does not mean that every time you are emotionally low your immune system will be weakened. Nor does it mean that every time you are happy that your immune system will be strong. There are many factors that can affect the immune system, of which emotion is only one of them.

Occasional anger, for example, is unlikely to cause any heart problems. Despite the evidence of the effects of anger on the heart, even regular anger may not be unhealthy, providing a well-needed emotional release valve for some people. Similarly, the effects of care, compassion, or appreciation, for instance, may not make everyone healthy.

But in general, due to the body-mind relationship, a consistently healthy mind will have a positive influence upon health. So whatever you can do in your life to improve your mental and emotional health, whether that is adopting a more positive attitude to life, meditating, laughing, choosing to appreciate people and life, choosing to be more caring and compassionate, or talking through any issues and pain with a friend, colleague, or therapist, there will most likely be benefits to your health.

The choice is yours!

2

The Power of Faith

The Placebo Effect

If you had a headache and a doctor gave you a medicine, telling you that it was a good painkiller, your headache would probably go away shortly after taking the tablet.

But it wouldn't really matter whether the doctor gave you a painkiller or a potato, if you believed that it was a painkiller then you would get pain relief. This is the placebo effect.

A placebo is a dummy medicine or treatment so there is nothing chemical in it that has healing powers. It is usually made to look and feel exactly like the drug being tested, so if the drug is a white tablet with a blue triangle on it then the placebo tablet is also white with a blue triangle on it.

Placebos are used in lots of medical trials around the world because they are not supposed to heal, therefore any curing that gets done can be credited to the medicine. In this way, researchers can prove that their new medicine works. But in practice, people do get healed when they take placebos.

The effect has been shown to cure anywhere between ten percent and one hundred percent of people, depending upon the nature of the trial and the type of illness being studied. For some diseases the placebo effect is low and for others it is high.

Say a medical trial was set up to determine how good a new drug for colds and flu was. It might involve a thousand people. Five hundred of them would get the drug and the other five hundred get the placebo. And just so there are no special treatments from the medical staff administering the tablets, no one knows who gets what. Neither the patients nor the medical staff.

During the course of the study, which might run for several months, information about the number and severity of episodes of colds and flu would be collected from each person, and then scientists would compare the symptoms of people who received the drug against those who received the placebo.

They might find that there were fewer symptoms in four hundred out of the five hundred people who received the drug, but they might also discover that there were fewer symptoms in three hundred who got the placebo. So there was clearly something in the way that the people on placebo were thinking or feeling that caused their bodies to heal.

It makes you wonder how many of the people who received the drug were actually cured by the placebo effect. Did the drug cure them or was it their faith in the drug?

It also makes you wonder how many times in the past your recovery from an illness had more to do with your belief in the medicine, or in the doctor, than in the medicine you were given. This is one of the reasons why a medicine might work well for one person but not for another.

One person might have more faith in the medicine than the other.

Placebo effects like these happen every day in hospitals, in doctor's surgeries, and at home. Snake oil might be a legitimate cure after all. It was great in its day because people believed in it. Some modern drugs are no better or worse.

Some doctors believe that it is important to give a patient a new drug while it is still considered the 'in thing' because once another new drug appears on the scene, the previous one seems to lose much of its miraculous healing power. And it's not because the medicine stops working but because people stop believing in it, especially because the new one is advertised to be an 'all singing all dancing wonder pill'.

Time has revealed that many miraculous medicines of the past were later found to have almost no curative powers of their own. But the patients who believed in them, and were cured by them, didn't know that at the time. It's just as well. Someone once said to me, *"Aerodynamically, a bumble bee shouldn't be able to fly but it doesn't know that."* It's just as well!

Taking faith out of the healing equation would, however, reveal many medicines to be very powerful but it is not possible to remove faith. The bottom line is that if you believe in a particular medicine, or in the doctor who prescribed it, then it is more likely to work for you. Similarly, if you don't believe in the medicine or in the doctor then there is a good chance that you will negate the medicine's power.

Some shamans in remote areas of the world are well aware of the power of an individual to cure her or himself and use that fact as a legitimate part of the 'whole person' treatment. Their ceremonies sometimes give the patient the feeling that they are being given 'the works'. The sick person totally buys into the treatment and their internal curative powers step in to do the work.

However this is not the only reason that such treatments work. The placebo effect is no more or less present in Shamanic medicine than it is in modern medicine. The shaman, for example, is also aware of the many herbs and combinations of plant essences, many of which modern drugs are modelled upon, that also have powerful curative properties, just as modern medicine uses drugs whose chemical action cures the body of disease. Shamans also use techniques to help them enter a higher state of consciousness where they are able to perceive the deeper mental, emotional, and spiritual nature of disease, allowing them to be more specific in their treatment.

There is more than one pathway to healing in the body. Molecules could move one way or the other during the process of recovery from illness. Faith could cause them to go left and medicines could cause them to go right. At the end of the day there's a healthy person. The placebo effect is powerful but so are plant essences, herbs, vitamins, minerals, and modern drugs.

There is a lot of dedication and genius from caring and compassionate scientists, whose goal is to make a difference in the world, that goes into the research and development of new treatments for most diseases. I should know because I used to be one of them. Scientists nowadays are able to chemically interrupt disease processes in ways that would even astound a rocket scientist.

The point is that there are many different types of medical treatment but since thoughts, feelings, and beliefs are so intimately entangled with the healing process it is probably wisest to go with that which you have most faith in.

Over the past 50 years a large number of scientific investigations have uncovered just how powerful healing can be when you believe in the treatment you are receiving.

Scientific Studies

Lots of research has been done on the placebo effect in recent years. Most scientists agree that it works because of two main factors: 1) A person's desire to be healed, and 2) their belief that they will be healed, either because they believe in the medicine or because they believe in the competency of the medical staff looking after them. Based upon the evidence discussed throughout this book, I would add a third: 3) the person's amount of 'feeling of certainty'. Having a lot of faith produces a strong feeling of certainty that they will be cured and having just a small amount of faith produces a small feeling of certainty, but it is the feeling that causes the healing.

In the bible it is written, "...*the blind men came to him. And Jesus says to them, Do you believe that I am able to do this? They say to him, Yea, Lord. Then he touched their eyes, saying, According to your faith, be it unto you. And their eyes were opened.*" **Mathew 9:28** [My emphasis in bold].

Science has since caught up a little with this teaching, revealing in numerous experiments that the degree to which you believe governs the rate you are healed. And the degree of belief is related to the degree of feeling of certainty.

In 1950, a scientific report was published in the 'Journal of Clinical Investigation' that described a powerful placebo effect in a group of thirty-three pregnant women who were having morning sickness.

The women took part in a trial where they were told that they would be given a drug that would stop their nausea and vomiting. This is what is called 'suggestion'. It was 'suggested' that the drug would work. To make the results even more precise the scientists asked the women to swallow a small instrument that would allow them to measure stomach contractions that came with the waves of nausea.

After they took the drug the women reported that their nausea and vomiting had stopped and the researchers also noted that the contractions, measured by the swallowed instruments, had also stopped. So the drug had been very successful.

But actually the women were not given a drug as they had been told. Instead they had been given a drug that should have made them even more sick, syrup of ipecac.

A strong desire to feel better (who wouldn't want to get rid of nausea?) coupled with a belief that the drug would work was able to override the powerful effects of a substance that should have made them worse. In this instance, a drug should have made molecules go left but faith was stronger and made them go right, figuratively speaking.

A similar type of study was conducted on asthma volunteers at the University of London in 1986.

A group of asthmatic volunteers were involved in a trial to apparently test a new drug. First they were told they would be given a substance that would cause their chests to constrict. So when they inhaled it through an inhaler their breathing became more difficult, as you would expect. Then the experiment was repeated, except that the new drug was given before the constricting substance, and they were told that it would protect them from it. In this instance the constricting substance had no effect.

However, in both cases the inhalers did not contain any such drugs. They contained water. Yet the volunteers had experienced chest constriction and expansion each time they used the inhalers. They believed that they were inhaling a chest constrictor or a new drug and this belief caused their bodies to act appropriately.

A very simple study, but one which clearly revealed the power of belief, was reported in 1996. It compared the effectiveness of capsules of different colours but which, unknown to the volunteers, contained the same substances.

A group of medical students were asked to take either the blue capsule or the pink one and were told that the capsules either contained a sedative or a stimulant, although in both cases they were chemically inert; they were placebos. But throughout the study it became apparent that the blue capsules were more powerful sedatives than the pink ones. It was probably because the volunteers associated the colour blue with calm and this association brought about a feeling of relaxation in their minds and then their bodies.

Similarly, a study of many different brands of aspirin tablets found that the ones with a red cross on them were the most powerful. Presumably it was because the red cross is usually associated with healing and brings about feelings of relief. These feelings would have caused healing in the body.

The power of the placebo effect is also easily noticeable in eating and drinking. On a number of occasions I have noticed that people with average health become sick more often once they start on a healthy diet and lifestyle. At first they feel great and their health improves, which is what should happen when a person improves their diet. But problems begin to arise as they learn more about what foods are considered good and which ones are not supposed to be so good. Now they look back at what they used to eat with horror, labelling most of it as unhealthy.

So now, whenever they have a slip-up from the healthy diet (which most of us do), eating something they now believe to be unhealthy, they are unconsciously telling themselves, "*I am unhealthy.*" This belief creates a placebo effect and the body simply reflects the belief as an illness. Previously, before they were enlightened to nutrition, eating that food would have caused no harm because the person did not know that it was bad for them.

It is sometimes not so much the food but our thoughts *about* food that cause us problems. Of course, there are foods that are generally accepted as nutritious and it is wise to eat them. There are also some that are not and eating lots of those every day might not be very clever. But the body is very resilient. Having the occasional French fry or piece of chocolate cake probably isn't going to make much difference to your health.

But a lot of people dwell on the thoughts of when they ate something fattening or sugary and so send their body lots of 'I am unhealthy' signals, which the body dutifully reproduces, forgetting the fact that almost everything else they ate was highly nutritious.

While the good food will have a health-giving effect, it is negated by the placebo effect of the 'I am unhealthy' mantra.

Our hearts and minds are so powerful that they can effortlessly override the effects of most food and drink we consume. If this happens to you then just keep reminding yourself that if you generally eat well then the majority of what you eat is nutritious and that the occasional slip-up probably won't do any harm.

Instant Healing

A few years ago, one of my friends had a heavy dose of the cold that gave her a headache, a blocked nose, and made her feel run down.

She had newly joined a charity that a group of friends and I operated, and was aware of a collective belief that we shared in 'hands-on' healing. Quite a few people in the group, for instance, were practising therapists.

At the time I also did some healing therapy work for people, usually family and friends, but as a scientist I was intrigued with how hands-on healing worked. As well as being a genuine therapy, I also recognised the presence of the patient's faith in the therapist and in the technique used.

My friend had never received a treatment but she really, really, believed in it because she had heard some remarkable stories.

On the day she spoke with me about her flu symptoms I felt genuine compassion for her and I offered to help. I had recognised her openness and faith, and the fact that she didn't know what a healing treatment consisted of, so I simply placed my hand on her forehead, gave her a little push and said out loud, with directness and conviction, *"Cold Cancel!"*

Her nose cleared and her headache vanished immediately!

I hadn't performed any special treatment. I simply recognised her faith that instant healing was possible and she did the rest. Her own belief caused a cascade of biological movements that made her instantly feel better, just in the same way that she could have taken a placebo tablet on the understanding that it was a powerful new drug known to have an immediate effect.

Molecules of Emotion

The power of the mind to cure is awesome and scientists have spent considerable time investigating it. In particular, they have studied tiny molecules called neuropeptides, which Professor Candace Pert labelled 'Molecules of Emotion' in her excellent book of the same name.

The name neuropeptide comes from their usual presence in the brain (neuro) and that they are made up of peptide units, which are parts of proteins.

The field of mind-body research has been active for many years, but it saw sudden growth in the 1970's when scientists discovered how mind-altering opiates like heroin, cocaine, and morphine worked. These addictive substances affected people's emotions.

A number of scientists had made the assumption that for opiates to affect the mind then they must interact with areas of the brain that control emotions. Such areas were well known at the time.

Have you ever seen those children's learning toys where there's coloured shapes and the children are supposed to fit them into the correct hole of the same shape on a small table? There is usually a square, a triangle, a circle, a star, perhaps a rectangle, and some other shapes, and each has it's own hole of the exact same shape on the table. Now imagine that when the child puts a correct shape in the hole then a green flashing light would go off.

Drugs and other chemicals interface with the brain in the same way. Each has its own hole on the table, or 'receptor' as its called in biology, and when a drug fits its receptor, instead of a flashing light the body switches on a particular function. In this way, when a drug fits its receptor the body can bring about healing.

A few scientists made the assumption that opiates had a specific 'hole', or receptor, in the brain's emotional areas. When opiates come along and fit into the hole, emotions are switched on and in this way they cause an emotional 'high'.

And it is now understood that the reverse is also true; that emotions produce neuropeptides. So it goes both ways; neuropeptides alter emotion and emotion produces neuropeptides. In mind-body science this is called 'bidirectional'.

In the modern history of mind-body science the existence of the opiate receptor was merely a theory but following its discovery in 1972 by Candace Pert and Sol Snyder, while at John Hopkins University, the entire field opened up.

Scientists reasoned that if these chemical opiates had a specific receptor that they fitted, then the body must have its own natural opiate, otherwise why would such a receptor exist?

Research soon uncovered it. It was identified at the University of Aberdeen, in Scotland, by John Hughes and Hans Kosterlitz and is known as endorphin.

It is the body's natural opiate that also gives you a 'high'. This is why sportspeople can become addicted to exercise, because endorphins are produced during intense exercise. The 'high' produced can be comparable to that of other addictive opiates.

It is now understood that neuropeptides are involved in a whole array of different bodily functions, from hormone regulation, to protein manufacture, to cellular repair upon injury, to memory storage, to pain management. And since neuropeptides are produced by emotion then all of these functions are affected by how a person feels.

Science now knows that there is an entire psychosomatic network connecting the body and mind, involving hundreds of neuropeptides and thousands of receptor locations all throughout the body. Any of a vast range of thoughts or feelings could cause a whole cascade of changes in a person's body. Thoughts and feeling basically 'light up' specific areas of the body.

Neuropeptides associated with any emotion will light up areas of the body where receptors for those neuropeptides are present, changing it in some way. And many neuropeptides have receptors all over the body so emotions are physically felt all over the body. They are subjective feelings but they are also real physical feelings.

For example, a 'gut feeling' is more than just a subjective feeling but also a real chemical movement in the gut where neuropeptide receptors reside. The feeling leads to production of specific neuropeptides in the brain and these light up specific receptors present in the gut, thereby allowing a person to physically feel an instinct.

Haven't you ever felt a full-body or spine tingle when you think a certain thought or feel a certain way, or when an idea just 'clicks'? Neuropeptides are simply fitting into receptors in those parts of the body.

Similarly, thoughts of care and compassion can induce changes in the immune system. They cause production of neuropeptides that light up receptors found on some immune cells, therefore switching them on.

If neuropeptides of compassion happened to have receptors in the big toe then compassion would light up the big toe.

Thoughts of appreciation can induce rhythm changes in the heart because neuropeptides associated with appreciation have receptors in the central nervous system. The whole body is psychosomatically wired to dance to any thought and emotion.

When a person has pain relief when they take a placebo, neuropeptides associated with faith (or feelings brought about by faith) must have receptors in the brain or where pain is felt.

In the 1970's, scientists began to study this and predicted that the neuropeptides might be opiates, or like opiates, because both morphine and endorphin are opiates and both provide pain relief.

The proof of this came in 1978 when scientists from the departments of Neurology, Physiology, and Oral Surgery, at UC San Francisco, published their research in the medical journal, 'The Lancet'.

Further studies since then by Fabrizio Benedetti and his co-workers, at the Department of Neuroscience at the University of

Torino Medical School in Italy, have concluded beyond all doubt that neuropeptides are responsible for pain relief when a person believes they are receiving a medicine.

To really nail it, researchers obtained brain scans using a technique called positron emission tomography (PET), which clearly showed that neuropeptides were around in the brain when a person on placebo was having pain relief. This research was published in 2002 in the journal, 'Science'.

So if you had a headache and the doctor gave you a painkiller or a potato, and you totally believed in his prescription, your headache would probably go away. The painkiller would work by fitting into pain receptors but the potato would work too because your faith in it would produce natural opiates which would also fit into the pain receptors.

Again, this is not to imply that medicines don't work. I have studied the biochemistry of how some of them work so I can tell you that they can be very powerful. But we all have the inherent ability to produce the same results through our faith.

Faith, hope, and determination can make a profound difference in the healing process. They might cure you completely, depending upon how much you can muster, or they might only make a small difference. But even a small difference is better than no difference. It might just be all you need.

One of the obstacles to healing is not realising the part you can play. Society causes us to believe that we must always seek cures outside of ourselves, dismissing 'mind over matter' as nonsense, but such a belief negates the body's natural healing process. Where the body may effortlessly recover from an ailment, our conditioned belief that we need a cure often stops it doing so.

Your beliefs can make a medicine work or neutralise it. Perhaps one day, when our faith is super strong, we will transcend the need for medicines altogether. But most people's faith is not super strong so it is wise to take whichever medicine a physician recommends.

Our understanding of the bodymind is growing every day. We are now recognising that even DNA, the building block of life and holder of the genetic code, dances to the tune of the mind.

3

DNA

DNA is frequently in the news amid reports of cloning and genetic modification of foods. Being the carrier of the genetic code, if scientists were to copy (clone) the code then they would produce a genetically identical animal or plant. Dolly the sheep was an example of an animal that was born from a cloned genetic code.

If they modified it then they would produce something that was similar, yet different; like a normal looking grain that was resistant to infection for instance. This is typical of some of the research that has been done on GM foods.

But while all of this research has been going on, a new area of DNA research called Psychosocial Genomics has emerged. A blend of psychology and genomics, its essence is that your DNA is influenced by how you think and feel. But before we go into that, here is a little lesson on DNA.

DNA is short for 'deoxyribonucleic acid', so you may understand why people prefer to call it DNA. Scientists have known for years that it has a 'double helix' structure, from the work of Crick and Watson, who received a Nobel Prize, and Rosalind Franklin, published back in 1953.

A double helix is what DNA looks like. Can you picture a spring in your mind? Say, a bedspring or a child's slinky spring? But instead of it being made of a single line of wire, imagine that a railway line has been coiled into a spring. So there are two lines that make up the spring and, just like a railway, picture that there are slats connecting the two strands. The two strands connected by the slats is a double helix.

The human genome project that you may have heard about was an international research programme set up to crack the genetic code. This meant that scientists wanted to know the exact chemical make-up of DNA.

You have probably heard of genes. Each gene is a small section of DNA whose presence causes you to have a particular physical characteristic, like eye colour or hair colour for instance. Imagine them as light bulbs, so that a coil of several thousand of them make up your DNA. In the human genome project, scientists wanted to know the exact sequence of light bulbs, as in which bulb came first, second, third, and so on.

Bet you didn't know that approximately 99.9% of our genes are the same for every person on earth. In other words, you and I have almost identical genes. Most people are under the impression that our genes are very different. Like having brown hair means that the person must have the brown hair gene, and having green eyes means having the green eyes gene. This makes logical sense but it is not entirely correct.

Much of the differences between us at birth actually have little to do with whether we have specific genes or not, because we have almost the same genes. Our differences at birth are mostly due to tiny variations in single genes.

Using the light bulb analogy, a single bulb could represent each gene but if you were to look inside each bulb you would see that it's element was made of a further thousand smaller bulbs. Scientists believe that the main differences between individuals are simply in the colour of just one of these thousand smaller bulbs inside a single gene. These variations are called single nucleotide polymorphisms (SNPs) and about 3 million are believed to exist.

However this is only part of the story because after birth, differences begin to emerge due to specific genes switching on in some people and off in others on account of their life experiences. So differences between people are produced by which genes are on and which ones are off.

Imagine a row of ten light bulbs. I might have bulbs 2, 4, 6, and 7 switched on with the rest off, while you might have numbers 4 and 6 switched off but bulb 8 switched on. In the human genome it is a little more complicated, with around 35,000 genes, but the light bulb analogy still stands.

Throughout life our numerous experiences and, more importantly, how we think and feel *about* these experiences, causes genes to switch on and off. And this produces significant biological differences between us. Learning has been proven to do this. Differences in what each person learns lead to differences in which genes are on and which ones are off.

The on and off-ness of genes is also a significant reason for the differences between us and other species of life. For example, there is a 98.5% similarity between our genes and those of chimpanzees. The differences are mostly down to which genes are on and which ones are off, and how long they are on or off for. Similarly, and unbelievably, 57% of our genes are shared with a cabbage, 51% with yeast, 50% with the worm, and 30% with the banana. Unbelievable, but true!

Our bodies are mostly composed of proteins, which are manufactured when genes switch on. They are the building blocks of our bodies, just as bricks are the building blocks of a house. So between species, it is mostly the same proteins that are present but just produced at different times and in different amounts. So just as the same set of bricks could be used to build a variety of different shapes and sizes of buildings, different combinations of genes being on and off can produce an infinite variety of species.

Because of the effect of our thoughts and feelings on our genes, it raises the question of how much can we alter our genes.

The effect varies between genes. In many cases, genetics may contribute around 50% (it can actually be anywhere between 0 – 100% depending upon the trait) of the person's makeup – physical and psychological – although this number varies depending upon the person's age and the physical, physiological, or behavioural trait in question. But the remaining 50% is open to the influence of the environment, which includes diet and lifestyle as well as thoughts and feelings. So genetics plays a significant role and so does life experience. Both nature and nurture are important.

For instance, if two people inherited almost identical genes (identical twins for instance) but lived in different environments, being exposed to different diets and life experiences, they would probably grow up to be different heights.

Scientific studies involving identical twins, for instance, have shown that height is around 80% heritable (a measure of the relative genetic influence) with the remaining 20% open to the environment. So while two people may have both inherited the same predisposition to be tall, their diets and daily experiences will have been the deciding factor as to what height they actually ended up.

So what this implies is that a person might never be stuck with a 'bad set of genes'. Almost any particular attribute or state of health could be changed, perhaps, with the aid of will power and faith. I believe that the question is not whether such a thing is possible or not, but how much will power and faith is required?

Genes and Visualisation

In a 1998 scientific paper Professor Eric Kandel, year 2000 Nobel Laureate in Physiology or Medicine, pointed out that all bodily functions are susceptible to social factors. His research focused upon the storage of memory and how each new experience causes genes to switch on so that proteins are manufactured to store the memory biologically.

When you experience anything like, say, meeting a new person or even enjoying a meal, it is stored in the brain as a memory, forming neural connections or, depending upon the intensity of the experience, forming brain cells (neurons) in a process known as neurogenesis.

Intense experiences like those of artistic or spiritual nature, or ones accompanied with a high emotional charge, produce neurons whereas normal everyday experiences produce simple neural connections. You could picture it as intense experiences producing balls and normal experiences producing thin fibres. But in each case it is not so much the experience but the thoughts and feelings *about* the experience, in other words, the mental and emotional processes during and after it, that cause this.

When something happens in a person's life, their thoughts and feelings about it switch on genes that construct whatever proteins or cellular components are required for its storage as a memory in the brain, biologically encoding it so to speak. (*I personally believe that memories are not just stored in the brain but that they have an equivalent all throughout the body, since the entire body is hardwired to feel every emotion. Its just that science hasn't looked anywhere else yet.*)

Any experience that is mentally and emotionally significant forms a strong, long lasting, memory because it is repeatedly played over and over in the mind. And as it is replayed in this way, the genes repeatedly express their information, over and over again, building up an indelibly etched memory, or biological equivalent, which can be a neuron if the experience is significant enough.

Think of a time when you had a powerful experience. Did you think about it for hours afterwards, even days? Did you daydream about it, even make up extra stuff in your mind? Of course you did.

It is this creative replaying, or daydreaming, that causes repetitive gene expression (switching on of the light bulb over and over and over again) that eventually produces neurons and neural connections. And if you think about it, replaying, or daydreaming, is visualisation.

So in other words visualisation (and the feelings associated with the images) inspires genes to switch on, causing the growth of proteins and cells. The more you visualise and the stronger the emotional charge accompanying it, the brighter the light bulb becomes, and the more proteins and cells you construct.

You might now understand why it was possible for the man described in the first chapter to completely regenerate his liver. His repetitive visualisations undoubtedly switched on specific genes, making the light bulb brighter if you like, that caused the construction of healthy liver cells.

In reality, our intentional and unintentional visualisations inspire DNA twenty-four hours a day, three hundred and sixty five days a year. We are simply unaware of the process. So we continually affect our genetic code and the nature of the effect is simply down to the nature of our thoughts, feelings, attitudes, beliefs, and intentions.

Put this into perspective in relation to health. When we are ill we tend to dwell on thoughts of the illness, which is normal because illness is usually unpleasant and difficult to remove attention from. But in doing this it is likely that we are actually helping to build new cells with a memory of disease. Our mental images, and their associated feelings of gloom, will switch on specific genes that build up diseased cells in our bodies.

On the other hand, if we release our emotional pains through talking with someone or having some sort of therapy then begin to dwell on positive, appreciative, thoughts and feelings then we will encourage the growth of healthy cells. This is why hypnosis has been shown to be a powerful tool in the healing arts and it is possibly also why releasing suppressed negative emotion can send cancers into regression.

In fact, spontaneous remission from cancer, which is where a cancer vanishes virtually overnight, has been theorised as a switching on of the interleukin-2 gene, on account of tremendous faith, hope, determination, visualisation, a complete change of belief system, or some other powerful experience. When turned on, this gene turbo-charges the immune system, causing a neutralisation of cancer cells and other harmful pathogens.

So even if a person inherited a tendency for an oncogene (cancer gene) to be switched on, a significant change of mind could switch it off, rendering the person healed.

If a person inherits an SNP that produces any disease I believe that it is possible that, with willpower and faith, they can create a new 'program' of genes switching on and off that would cancel it out.

This is not to say that it is easy to do so. Few individuals have demonstrated such ability. It simply means that it is possible. Our current understanding of this process is primitive, but it *does* suggest that such things *are* possible and that there is probably a way to harness the ability to perform such miracles at will. Some individuals probably unconsciously do it all the time. Perhaps this will be more commonplace at some point in the future.

Genes and Love

One of the most powerful effects of heart and mind on DNA that has been reported to date in the scientific journals, is the effect of love, or lack of it.

In 1995, while studying rat pups, researchers showed that when a mother's touch is deprived then there is a dramatic reduction in the levels of important growth hormones in the infant's bodies.

Growth hormones are the substances in the body that cause cells, organs, and individual body parts to grow so they are of prime importance in the bodies of children.

The researchers studied two genes called 'c-myc' and 'c-max', which switch on another gene called 'ornithine decarboxylase' (ODC) that is involved in the construction of growth hormones in the body. Maternal touch promotes switching on of c-myc and c-max, leading to normal growth of an infant.

However, the researchers discovered that if maternal touch was deprived for ten or fifteen minutes then there was a forty percent drop in ODC gene expression. Forty percent! That's a forty percent drop in growth hormone levels. In other words, deprivation of touch had a stunting effect on growth.

This might give you an idea of the importance of love. A mother's touch makes an infant feel loved and the love promotes its growth. When there is no loving touch, feelings of fear (the absence of love) are experienced and this suppresses its growth.

Love promotes growth and fear suppresses it!

But before you worry about laying your infant down for a short time, the scientists also discovered that if maternal touch was resumed then ODC over expressed by a factor of three hundred percent, producing elevated amounts of growth hormones, as if to make up for lost time. Nature, it seems, is not without a sense of balance.

Infants benefit from a range of experiences that don't always involve direct touch from a parent, for example when it is playing with toys. So it seems like nature has built this overcompensation into the process of evolution.

Some researchers have actually discovered that a positive, loving, environment in the home is ideal. While studying the brain, they discovered that the area known as the prefrontal lobes, at the front of the head just above the eyes, grows more pronounced if a child is brought up in such a positive, loving, household environment. When that child grows into an adult it has a well developed set of prefrontal lobes, and these are associated with it being able to comfortably express itself, being emotionally well adjusted, and being spiritually aware.

When a child is consistently deprived of love there can be a stunting effect on its growth and the prefrontal lobes don't fully develop. A child with underdeveloped prefrontal lobes often has difficulty with emotional expression later in life.

A number of social workers investigating neglected children have actually reported finding abnormally small children who were later found to have extremely low levels of growth hormones as well as having difficulty 'fitting in'. The feelings experienced by the children presumably switched off c-myc and c-max, thereby slowing the growth process. The condition is known as *'psychosocial dwarfism'* or *'non-organic failure-to-thrive'*.

Please note, however, that a person's size, in general, is not an indicator of how much love they received as a child. As we learned previously, around 80% of height is in the genes. Only 20% is influenced by environment and life experiences. The point is merely that the on-ness or off-ness of the genes is *influenced* by love and fear.

Genes and Determination

As we have learned, we are rarely stuck with a 'bad set of genes', so to speak. Our mental and physical abilities can be mastered through learning and practise. And as we learn and practise, our thoughts and feelings switch on genes that help us to master whatever we are focusing upon. Similarly, our general state of health can be improved when we are determined to recover from an illness, or when we are visualising ourselves well.

My mum enjoyed jumping when she was a child. She loved jumping so much that she became really good at the high jump as a teenager and performed excellently at the county sports championships. For years afterwards she talked about her memories of jumping over the clothes ropes in her back garden every evening, and the joy she felt from it. I was often moved by the excitement in her voice as she vividly recounted these experiences, acting out the jumping motions on the sitting room floor.

As I grew up I loved to watch athletics on the TV with my family, particularly the Olympic Games. I would often daydream about being an athlete and competing in a major championship. In my mid twenties I tried out for the sprint team in a large UK athletics club called Sale Harriers Manchester but although I was quite fast I wasn't good enough to make the team. A few days later I was at the track by myself, playing around at jumping into the sand pit.

After several jumps the head of the club approached me. He had been watching me and wondered who I was, because I was a new face at the track. He asked how far I could jump so I paced out my last jump and said it looked to be about six and a half metres, which is about twenty-one and a half feet. He was visibly impressed and asked me to come to the track the following evening because that's when the long jump squad train, under the coaching of Terry Davidson. He wanted me to join the club as a long jumper, so I did. And I became very good at it.

Within a month or two, under Terry's coaching, I was one of the top long jumpers in Scotland, but prior to Sale Harriers Manchester I had never done a day's formal jump training in my life. Most of my training had been mental and emotional daydreaming.

There is most likely a 'jumping gene' or a set of genes that motivate a person to want to jump and thus develop stronger and more elastic muscles. I may have been born with the genes turned on, but then again I may not. They might have simply been turned on because of the thoughts, feelings, and motivations I was exposed to through my mum's love of jumping.

These mental and emotional experiences would have written and new genetic program, switching on specific genes that caused my muscles to develop and perform in an appropriate way. My ability would have been independent of whether I had inherited 'athletic genes' or not.

If you think about it, it is doubtful that every Olympic medallist will have been born with 'athletic genes'. In the history of such major championships, I believe that numerous genes have been encouraged to switch on through sheer determination and will power.

Any of us have the capacity to become pretty much anything we desire because we have all of the genes in the gene pool and they are all susceptible to mental and emotional influence. The question is simply, what are you motivated to become? There are probably no limits to what any of us can be.

All of us have the 'Olympic athlete gene' waiting to be expressed, and the 'great artist', 'sculptor', 'musician', 'actor, 'scientist', 'writer', 'teacher', 'peacemaker', 'lover', 'parent', 'empathic', 'genius', and 'healer gene'. It's all in your DNA, just waiting for you to want it and have faith that you can Be it.

Many people's latent abilities are obstructed by their belief that they can't do something. Who says you can't? You can!

Amazing abilities are latent within all of us. Everyone can live their dreams, regardless of past conditions or performances of family members. Anyone can have a desire and a little faith, and that might just be all that is needed.

Look to what's in your heart!

4

The Power of Intention

Already we have learned that our thoughts and feelings affect our health, even altering our genes, and this happens 24 hours a day, 365 days a year, mostly without our knowledge of what is happening.

But the same can be done with conscious knowledge. The scientific journals contain hundreds of research papers that show that we can use mental techniques to affect our bodies and other people's bodies, and even affect plants and other organisms. Visualisation, for instance, where you might create a mental picture of a person in full health, can speed up healing in any area of the body.

The results of visualisation are not always obvious because many people are looking for the 'instant fix'. Most think that if they visualise when they have an illness then it should go away right away. It should! But there are very few people who hold strong enough beliefs to make it so.

Instead many of us do the opposite. Our beliefs that it is not possible are often just as strong as our beliefs that it is possible and so we interfere with the healing process. We take two steps back for every three we take forward and eventually the strongest belief wins.

The result is that visualisation only *appears* to have small effects. But even so, a small effect is better than no effect.

No matter what ache, pain, or illness you might ever experience, intend to get better. Determination coupled with hope and a little faith can move mountains. If a placebo effect exists for an illness or pain then the body clearly has the ability to heal it if we believe, hope, or are determined enough. There is no condition in the body that is not susceptible to will-power and faith. Most of us know of people whose resolve has overturned huge odds.

Our thoughts and feelings can affect other people's bodies too. Have you ever noticed that if you are in a bad mood then you quickly affect the mood of everyone around you? And the same is true when you are in a good mood. You might even have noticed how some people have this effect on you. These are example of how your thoughts and feelings have affected another person, or vice versa.

If you affect a person's mood then you also affect their biochemistry because the body and mind are intertwined. Just as your mood affects your body, their mood affects theirs. If you have altered their mood then you have affected their biology in an indirect way. Therefore, you can intentionally affect someone's health in a positive way.

For example, if you were to generate a warm feeling of appreciation for a person when you are in their company, they will sense it and their feelings will have healing effects throughout their bodies. You will have had a positive effect upon them. So in a very real sense love heals.

You can even go further and do direct healing work on a person through visualisation, and this usually works independently of your effect on their mood.

Scientific studies imply that if someone is sick or in pain you can will them to get better, for instance, and your hopes and intentions will help them. This happens all the time, only we rarely notice the role our intentions played in their recovery, instead putting recoveries solely down to specific medicines, food, or even luck. Of course, medical treatment and nutrition will have had a powerful effect but so, too, has your will power.

However, please note that there are times in some people's lives when it is just 'their time' and all you can hope for is that your intentions help give them some comfort in the final stages.

To focus your willpower you can actively visualise a person in perfect health, who has an ache or pain, or is sick. You can even put your hands on them while imagining this.

Over the last few years there has been a rapid rise in the number of practitioners of healing techniques within and outside of the sphere of complementary and alternative medicine. This is where a therapist lays his or her hands upon you and conducts healing. In fact there are a far greater number of practitioners of techniques like Therapeutic Touch and Reiki, in some countries, than there are doctors.

Such practitioners are trained to place their hands on, or just above, an area to be healed. Many use visualisation techniques while others don't visualise, simply trusting that healing is taking place. I know a number of people who have testified to feeling incredibly relaxed during and after a session, and whose physical, mental, emotional, or spiritual condition has cleared up shortly afterwards.

Anyone can perform healing on another person. Proper training can teach anatomy, physiology and diagnosis, the biological and medical consequences of where to place your hands, where specific organs are, as well as teach about medical science and ethics, but anyone can help another person by simply compassionately willing them to recover. On the note of ethics, I prefer to always ask a person's permission before I visualise them.

All that is required is compassion, a willingness to help, and a little faith that you might indeed be helping in some way. Belief of some of the scientific proof of healing will provide a little of the faith so you're half way there.

Scientists have studied some of these therapies and have proven how effective they can be.

In the 1960's Dr Bernard Grad, of McGill University in Montreal, measured the effects of healing touch on mice.

He asked a healer named Oscar Estebanay to place his hands, every day, upon individual goitrous mice in a selected group to see if Mr Estebanay could speed up healing in those mice, relative to others that he wasn't to perform healing upon. Over the course of the study Dr Grad indeed found that Mr Estebanay had slowed down the rate of development of goitre in the mice that he touched.

In a similar way he studied the effects of a healer's touch on the rate of healing of skin wounds on mice. After daily healing treatments he discovered that the wounds closed up much faster on the mice that had been handled by the healer.

In 1972 the same healer was involved in a study that even looked at the effect of healing touch on some enzymes held in a jar.

Enzymes are molecules that the body uses to transform one substance into another. For example, many are involved in digesting food where they convert it, or break it down, into other substances that the body can use.

The study found that daily healing treatments of the enzyme 'trypsin', over a three-week period, improved its performance in converting substances.

A study conducted in 1999, by Toni Bunnell at the University of Hull in the UK, studied the effect of healing touch on another enzyme, called 'pepsin'. Over a series of twenty trials, she found that the healer speeded up the rate that it carried out its 'converting'.

Unlike physical touch, clearly there is some sort of transfer of energy through the air from the healer to the enzymes, just as heat can pass from people to objects they hold. However science has proven that its not just heat that transfers during healing treatments.

Similarly, an earlier 1984 study looked at the effects of healing on the mutation of live bacteria, something that occurs quite naturally in the human body.

The bacteria Escherichia Coli, or E-coli as it is more commonly known, mutates from one strain, known as *lac*-negative, into another strain, *lac*-positive.

Fifty-two people were involved in the study and were given nine tubes each, containing a mixture of both the negative and positive strains. Each person was to hold the tubes in their hands then try to mentally speed up mutation in three tubes, slow down mutation in another three, and leave the last three alone to serve as controls.

The results were highly significant. The researchers discovered that the tubes where the subjects had tried to speed up mutation had much more *lac*-positive E-coli than in the control samples. The subjects had speeded up the mutation, producing more *lac*-positive E-coli in the allotted time.

They also found that there was much less *lac*-positive E-coli in the tubes where the subjects had attempted to slow down mutation.

Healing also works with plants. In one of Dr Grad's experiments, he damaged a set of barley seeds by watering them with salt water. Half of them, however, had been watered with salt water that had been held for a few moments by a healer, while the other half of them were watered with salt water that hadn't been held. He then dried the seeds in an oven then watered them every day with ordinary water.

At the end of the experiment he discovered that the seeds that had been watered with the salt water held by the healer grew much faster than the seeds that had been watered with 'unhealed' saltwater. Somehow there had been a transfer of energy from the healer into the water and it was able to cancel out the damaging effects of the salt water.

You have probably heard of the 'old wives tale' that talking to your plants makes them grow better. Scientific evidence shows that this tale should be taken quite literally. In his book, "Autobiography of a Yogi", Paramahansa Yogananda describes some of the work of Luther Burbank.

Yogananda noticed that Mr Burbank's garden had cactus plants with no thorns, and this intrigued him to ask about them. When they were first planted, Yogananda was told, the cacti did have thorns, but Mr Burbank spoke kindly and tenderly to them on a regular basis, explaining to them that they didn't need their thorns any more because he harboured no intentions of ever harming them. Gradually the cacti gave up their thorns!

I once visited my friends Andrea, Seth, Kenny, and Pamela, and was quite impressed by the abnormal size of some of their window plants. Andrea told me that she had been giving them Reiki every day since they were seeds. It had clearly helped their growth.

I am sure that many people reading this right now have noticed that their plants grow better when they are kind to them, just as humans do.

Every day, most of us come into contact with lots of people; family members, colleagues, other people that we know, and many people that we don't know. There is clear scientific evidence that indicates that your thoughts about them have an effect upon them.

Do you appreciate them or do you harbour anger or resentments towards them?

I have noticed that I can sometimes effortlessly change the atmosphere in a room simply by thinking how much I appreciate each person, and feeling the appreciation. Quite often there's a profound transformation, right before my eyes, within a few minutes. A cold, or even openly hostile, environment can be transformed into a warm, loving, happy, peaceful, or forgiving one.

So every time you think, smile, or say something nice to a person your intentions may be touching her or him in some way.

A kind thought, a smile, or a few genuinely kinds words cost nothing but they can go a very long way.

Go with the Flow

When people are being treated, in a healing environment, with someone laying their hands upon them, there must be a flow of energy from the healer into the patient, and this must be affected by intentions.

This knowledge is quite new in the west but it has been well known for thousands of years in the east. Ancient healing traditions in China and India, for instance, are based upon the flow of a vital and health-giving energy around the body. This energy is called by many names in many cultures but the most common are: qi (chee), prana, and life-force.

These traditions teach that the body requires qi to function. A healthy body contains lots of qi and it flows smoothly throughout it, just as blood flows through veins.

When a person is sick the flow of qi might be blocked, just as a body would become sick if blood flow was blocked.

It is well known that a blockage in the blood flow to the heart, for instance, can cause a heart attack. In the same way, a blockage in the flow of qi can introduce the body to a whole range of illnesses by depriving an organ of its vital energy.

Think of it this way: If you were to build a dam on a river, blocking it, then people who needed water downstream would not get enough to drink and to nourish their crops. In the same way, if the flow of qi along a particular 'river', or 'meridian' as it is called, is blocked then any organ that usually receives qi from that meridian would not get the supply it needs so its health would suffer.

Common sense says that to heal an organ that is not getting enough qi, you would need to remove the blockage.

This is what acupuncture and many other complementary and alternative therapies try to do. Acupuncturists place needles on meridians at specific locations, known as acupuncture points, that help to stimulate the flow of qi so that it dissolves the blockages.

Up until recently western science hadn't accepted the existence of acupuncture points or meridians but relatively recent scientific studies have changed that outlook. Now, a large number of modern medical practices list acupuncture as a genuine treatment.

For example, even though microscopes can't see them, on points of the body that have been identified as acupuncture points scientists have measured ten to twenty-fold differences in electrical resistance compared to points, only a centimetre or two away, which are not acupuncture points.

They have also discovered different amounts of key chemicals at these points. They have even been able to inject radioactive substances into acupuncture points and then follow their flow around the body, creating a map, which was found to be identical to the ones drawn up by ancient Chinese and Vedic practitioners.

Earlier in the book we learned that emotions can be stored anywhere in the body, because neuropeptides associated with those emotions have receptors all over, and that a storage of emotional pain can cause disease. Stores of negative emotions, then, might also be blocking the natural flow of qi into an organ or other body part, just as a storage of, say, fat or cholesterol might block blood flow to the heart.

As we also learned, suppressed negative emotions can be expressed and resolved, which is a process that must also, therefore, clear the qi blockages.

Qi blockages can also be removed by any medical treatment or therapy that restores the natural flow, often causing a release of previously blocked emotion, just as unblocking a dam would result in a sudden deluge of water downstream. This is why acupuncture, and other energy therapies like Reiki or Shen, for instance, sometimes causes patients to laugh or cry.

Several years ago I had an acupuncture treatment at a time in my life when I was having difficult mental and emotional challenges. As is normal at such times I was taking life very seriously, perhaps a bit too seriously and forgetting to see the lighter side. After a few minutes of having needles placed in me I began to laugh. I don't think I'd laughed for several weeks before then so it was quite a relief. As the treatment removed a blockage of qi it also cleared a blockage of emotion that I had stored up. The acupuncture treatment was a highly beneficial and well-needed therapy.

A simple exercise that I have found useful in clearing blockages is as follows: Joining my hands together in the prayer position, I focus my attention on my right hand and try to become aware of what it feels like. I then mentally move that feeling up through the wrist, up the forearm, to the elbow. Then up the bicep to the shoulder, along to the neck, through the neck, out the other side to the left shoulder, and down the left side to the left hand, and through to the right hand as the circuit begins again. When I've done several circuits I then mentally move the flow anywhere in my body, through any blockages or areas where there are any problems.

What I am doing is becoming aware of qi in my body and mentally encouraging some of its movement to where I want it to go. This technique can be used to direct energy and healing intention through any diseased or painful part of the body, helping it to heal.

Some healing techniques, like this one, guide qi to flow through blockages in the hope that the passage of energy might unblock them, just as the rapid flow of water along a blocked pipe, for example, might dislodge the debris that is blocking it.

A scientific study into stroke investigating the technique known as qigong, a practise that uses intention to direct qi around the body, was performed over a thirty-year period and involved two hundred and forty two hypertensive patients. Half of the patients performed thirty minutes of qigong twice daily and the other half did not.

The number of patients who experienced a stroke in the group who didn't practise qi-gong was around forty percent (there is a well known link between hypertension and stroke). But in a clear demonstration of the power of qigong, in the group who practised it the figure was only twenty percent. Regular practise had halved the number of patients having a stroke.

An additional bonus of the experiment was that the group who practised qigong used their medication less, and thirty percent of them stopped their medication altogether.

Another research project showed that qigong was of enormous benefit to people with cancer. It involved one hundred and twenty cancer patients, ninety of whom practised two hours of qigong a day for three to six months. During the course of the study all patients received medication for the cancers.

In the qigong practising group physical strength increased by eighty percent, yet by only ten percent in the other group.

Appetite increased in sixty percent of the group who regularly practised qigong, but only by ten percent in the non-qigong group. Following this, a significant weight gain was measured in sixty percent of the qigong group but in only fifteen percent of the non-qigong group.

And lastly, the strength of the immune system increased by fifteen percent in the qigong group but reduced by twenty percent in the group who did not practise qigong. It was likely that the practice of qigong helped to unblock some storages of suppressed emotion as well as increase the amount of vital energy being supplied to all of the organs.

Intention is very powerful. We intend things all throughout the day, most of the times not even being aware of what we are intending. But every one of your intentions goes somewhere and quite likely, as you will learn later in the book, if you are thinking of a specific person it will be going right to them, just as a healing intention will go right where you want it to in your body.

This is good if your intentions are kind, compassionate, appreciative, or even uplifting, because you will be helping the person in some way, but how often do you slip into thinking about how someone has offended you, or hurt you in some way, or how you disapprove of their behaviours? What effect do you think your intentions will be having then?

It can do more good to find it in yourself to forgive people, or to accept them just as they are, than to send harmful intentions to them. How would you feel if you knew that someone was judging you unfairly without knowing the 'real' you, or thinking angry thoughts about you for something you may or may not have meant to do?

Every person you have ever interacted with might be a good father or mother, husband or wife, son or daughter, or friend, and is dearly loved by someone, just as you are. The way you might have experienced this person is not who they really are, it is just how you have experienced them.

Try to be fair to people. You will probably never know the real reasons why a person might have behaved in a certain way. You have probably behaved less than perfectly on at least one occasion of you life and it wouldn't be fair of someone to judge you for life on that one example.

You can shield yourself from unwanted intentions, and that works fine, but you will discover that if you are genuinely nice to people and think highly of them, seeing the best in them, then there won't be a need to. What you give out always comes back to you, in one form or another.

Being genuinely good to people is a good way to improve your overall health. My dear friend Margaret McCathie, after suffering years of depression and even attempting suicide, was told by Dr Patch Adams (known for the Hollywood film, 'Patch Adams') to "*Go out and serve and see your depression lift.*" She did so and within a few months her depression had indeed lifted and she is now a Professional Laughter Therapist, inspiring others to find their inner joy through service, laughter and kindness. The effect she has on people is extraordinary.

The gift of joy she gave to people was returned to her, not only lifting her out of depression but also helping to evolve her into an abundant embodiment of happiness.

5

Good Vibrations

Vibrations in Water

Dr Grad's experiments with barley seeds clearly showed that energy had been transferred, or somehow imprinted, into water. The effect of the healer holding the salt water was able to override the damaging effect of the salt on the seeds. You might want to think a few kind thoughts the next time you are about to drink a glass of water. Could it be that your intentions will colour it and you will nourish your body in a way you might never have imagined?

Some scientists have studied how water changes in accordance with thoughts and emotions. For instance Professor William Tiller, who is emeritus professor of materials science at Stanford University, has analysed water that has been held by a healer and detected subtle changes in it.

In a glass of water the atoms (H-O-H) vibrate, constantly coming together and bouncing apart. They also bend, stretch, spin, and twist.

Professor Tiller and others have measured changes in some of these movements in water when a healer has held the water, focused thoughts upon it, or felt strong emotions around it. Their results suggest that your own thoughts and feelings affect water in this way, altering its vibrations.

During a thanksgiving meal with some friends a few years ago, which included Dr Glen Rein of the Quantum Biology Research labs in New York, a talented scientist who also conducted some of the Institute of Heartmath's research, I learned that Dr Rein had even placed DNA in a jar containing water that has been held or focused upon and then detected changes in its conformation.

Imagine you are sitting cross-legged on a chair and then someone switches on a heater in the room. It gets so warm that you feel uncomfortable so you change your seating position and place your feet flat on the floor. Dr Rein showed that DNA changes the way it 'sits' when it gets placed in water that a healer has held or focused intention upon. This is what is called 'changes in conformation' of DNA.

The body is composed of about 70% water and contains thousands of miles of DNA. This research would suggest that both the water and your DNA might be constantly affected by what you think about and how you feel. Together with modern research in psychosocial genomics, there is little doubt that qualities of heart and mind have an effect upon our DNA.

Also, your intentions towards other people will affect the water in their bodies too, and their DNA. Of course the effects are very small and subtle. Loving a person may not enlighten them and a dislike of a person is not going to switch on genes that make them grow an extra arm out of their forehead. But continued intentions may build up over time just as, say, trace chemical contaminants in food build up over time and can have toxic consequences.

On the positive side, consistently kind and appreciative intentions towards people will have a long-term beneficial effect upon them. It might make little difference, or it might make a lot, but even a little difference in the right direction is better than a little difference in the wrong direction. How are your intentions towards people?

Knowing the effects of thoughts and feelings on it, water can be a programmable medicine. For instance, you could write the word 'appreciation' on a label and stick it to a bottle or glass of water before you drink from it. The word will unconsciously trigger a thought or emotion in you every time you drink from it, however small, and this will 'colour' the water, probably inspiring internal coherence in your body.

It might also make you feel more appreciative towards yourself or others. You could try it with 'love', 'peace', 'happiness', 'joy', 'forgiveness', 'passion', 'kindness', or even 'healing' if you want to bring more healing into your body. You can be creative. Any quality of intention you wish to add to your body can be written on a label and stuck to the bottle or glass. The effects may be subtle or significant and will most likely depend on what you believe!

Chemical Imprints in water

Some aspects of homeopathic medicine and vibrational medicine utilise the transfer of energy into water.

Plant essences, like Bach Flower Remedies for example, fall into the category because they rely, in part, on the vibrations (bending, stretching, spinning, twisting) of the substances extracted from the plants, to be transferred into water.

Manufacture of these medicines uses homeopathic 'succussion' techniques where the plant leaf or flower is boiled up then diluted with water or alcohol. It is then shaken vigorously while making a series of successive dilutions. Each episode of shaking is called succussion and is believed to 'imprint' the vibrational energy of the leaf or flower into the water.

There is also a degree of symbolism and emotion brought about by the image of certain flowers and plants and it is believed that the emotional energy associated with these is also imprinted into the water.

The same kind of thing has been done with certain types of rocks or crystals that have been shown to possess paramagnetic qualities, or believed to absorb qi or intention. Shaking the rocks, or ground up chunks of them, in water and making successive dilutions is believed to imprint the magnetism or qi into the water, producing medicines that have been shown to have significant health enhancing effects upon the body, and even on plants.

For example, in some 'rough' and unpublished experiments of my own I have found that some rocks and crystals (particularly ground up rose quartz) accelerate the rate of germination and growth of seeds of cress.

Some therapists imprint water with loving intentions, through holding it while focusing on a feeling of genuine love and 'concentrating' it with successive dilutions. The patient then receives a concentrated burst of love at a deep level in their body, often producing miraculous results. One of the real advantages of this type of medicine is that the effects go beyond the physical body and have healing effects on emotions and on spiritual challenges, which are frequently the underlying causes of disease in the body.

Relatively recent, accidental, research stumbled upon scientific proof of the power of vibrational medicine.

During research into allergies Professor Jacques Benveniste, while research director at the French National Institute for Health and Medical Research, was studying the effect of chemical solutions of allergens on white blood cells of the immune system.

A chemical solution is basically a substance dissolved in water, alcohol, or some other solvent. For example a chemical solution of salt would be a spoonful of salt in a glass of water. A chemical solution of allergens is allergens dissolved in water, or dissolved in water plus something else like alcohol.

However one of his students accidentally over-diluted a solution so much that, theoretically, it should not have been able to do anything to the immune system because there weren't enough allergen molecules left in the solution. In fact they eventually diluted it so much that there was no theoretical possibility of their being even a single molecule of allergen present, so it should have had no effect on the white blood cells. Yet it did. And significantly so! The diluted solution affected the immune system as much as the original chemical solution did. Some of the vibrational energy of the allergen must have been imprinted into the water during the dilution process.

Professor Benveniste and his team had accidentally proven vibrational medicine.

Amid a degree of controversy, the research was reported in 1988 in the highly prestigious journal 'Nature', stimulating a degree of scientific debate into homeopathy and, in the eyes of many, lending genuine credibility to homeopathic medicine because homeopathy relies on using very dilute quantities of substances to have an effect on the body. One of the ways in which some homeopathic medicines work, although not the only way, is that vibrational energy of a substance is imprinted into a solvent during the succussion process.

If you were to clap your hands, the air around them would get disturbed. The air would appear to be pulsating, vibrating. Someone moving close to you might feel the vibrations as a breeze. In a similar fashion, water feels the vibrations of the stretching, twisting, and bouncing of molecules and substances dissolved in it.

Common sense would tell you that if you could reproduce the same vibrations in another way then you could 'fake' a chemical medicine.

Professor Benveniste and his team accomplished this. In several experiments they recorded the vibrations of some chemical substances onto CD and discovered, by playing the CD instead of using the chemical, that they could trigger biological changes to the same degree that they could achieve using the chemical substances.

Over a series of experiments, for instance, they adjusted the amount of blood pumping through a heart depending upon what recording they played.

If, for example, they played the recording of a chemical called acetylcholine, which is known to dilate blood vessels, then more blood would pump through the heart.

If they injected a real chemical solution of acetylcholine they got the same results. It didn't matter to the heart whether it received a chemical substance or just the energy vibrations from the substance.

The digitised signal increased blood flow by 21.5% and the chemical solution increased it by 21.3%. Almost identical.

To further demonstrate the scale of their discoveries they even recorded a set of chemical vibrations and sent them by e-mail from the USA to their laboratory in France, downloaded the signal and played it to an organism. Astonishingly, the signal produced biological changes as much as a chemical solution. At the current time of writing (2005), this research has not been fully embraced by the scientific community but, as is often the case with paradigm shifting discoveries, I predict that 'Digital Biology', as it is called, will eventually have a huge impact upon medical science.

If you think about it, a similar thing happens when you play music. All sounds are vibrations. Hearing requires vibrations triggering biology in your ear. So all sounds most likely affect your body to some extent, just as Professor Benveniste's CDs do. Playing classical music beside a person, for instance, can alter their mood, which involves a movement of neuropeptides, and might even boost their immune system, smooth the rhythms of their heart, and switch on and off sets of genes.

Words and musical sounds are vibrations in space, as is digitised signals, while vibrational medicines are simply vibrations in water. But a vibration is a vibration. It's only the medium they are transmitted in that is different. All vibrations affect us. Some effects are obvious and some are not so obvious.

You probably haven't considered it but every word you speak, on account of its vibrations, affects your body and it affects the body of any person you speak it to.

Sound & Meaning

Spiritual mystics have known, and taught, for thousands of years that sounds can have profound health-giving effects on the body. Some spiritual mystics have said that the sounds 'Ah' and 'O' are primordial sounds, the sounds of creation, and so either is found in the name of the creator in just about every culture in the world: God, Jehovah, Yahweh, Ra, to name a few. In The New Testament of The Bible, the Gospel of John begins with, *"In the beginning was the Word and the Word was with God, and the Word was God."* **John 1:1**. Creation, according to John, began with the Word – a sound vibration!

A meditation technique known as the Japa meditation involves vocalising the sound of the creator, whatever that may be in your culture, over and over again. It is believed to bring the meditator into conscious contact with the creator and so reveal the spirit.

You may have noticed that certain pieces of music affect your mood. Some have a relaxing effect on your body and mind while other pieces have a stimulating effect, each causing a crescendo of biological interactions. Some even give you 'flashbacks' of past experiences, and flashbacks are visualisations so they probably alter the expression of several sets of genes and affect your immune system in a manner depending upon whether you regard the memories as good or bad.

A scientific study published in 1996, in the scientific journal 'Stress Medicine', directly showed how certain pieces of music could affect the immune system. They found that some pieces increased levels of the immune system's salivary immunoglobulin

A (remember that?). One particular piece used in the experiment increased s-IgA levels by 55%.

Earlier we learned that a feeling of appreciation could raise s-IgA levels. The scientists put the two together, asking the test subjects to think 'appreciation' while a specific piece of music was played, and the levels of s-IgA went up by 141%. Quite a therapy!

A study, published in 2002 in the journal 'Alternative Therapies', reported that the immune system was also boosted by certain types of drumming and also reported that there was a reduction in the levels of some stress hormones during the experiment.

Drumming is used by some shamans to help them enter into an altered state of consciousness. The vibrating sound of the drumming produces sound vibrations (waves) which presumably causes production of mind-altering opiate-type neuropeptides that fit into receptors in the emotional areas of the brain. Prolonged drumming probably even involves a number of genes being switched on and off.

But it is not only music that has this effect. A kind word said to someone can be music to their ears and make them feel comforted, and such a comforting feeling will have a positive effect on their health.

The meaning of your words are clearly important because it triggers thoughts, feelings, and mental images depending upon how the person feels about what you say to them. The words 'I love you', for instance, may mean a lot to the person you say them to and can cause him or her to feel fantastic, and this will have knock-on health promoting effects.

But the actual sound of the words, the vibrations of the vowel and consonant sounds, also affect the body and this occurs independent of its meaning. The sound of the word 'love', for example, contributes to its biological effects as well as its meaning does. So words affect us on two levels, through what they mean to us and through the vibrating sound of their pronunciation.

So a word is more than a mere description of something, it is a set of vibrations in space and these vibrate at various levels throughout your body. Some may be felt on the skin, like the way you can 'feel' the vibrating sound of music when you stand close to a loud speaker, some may resonate with internal organs and, almost certainly, with the chemical bonds between atoms in DNA and in some of the vital proteins and enzymes in your body.

Have you heard of how the human voice can shatter glass? Ella Fitzgerald, while holding a specific vocal note, could shatter nearby wine glasses. The sound resonated with the internal structure of the glass, eventually causing it to explode into tiny pieces. In a similar way, ultrasound can be used to deliver a knockout blow to kidney stones, shattering them into tiny pieces that can easily be eliminated from the body. Recently, at Borders General Hospital in Scotland, Dr Syme reported significant reduction of stroke symptoms using ultrasound.

Could it be possible, then, for human vocal sound to have a positive effect upon serious disease in the human body?

I watched a video where three doctors from the Huaxia Zhineng Qigong Clinic and Training Centre in Qinhaungdao, China, demonstrated this. They stood behind a woman who had a cancerous tumour in her bladder that was approximately three inches wide, and a real-time ultrasound scan of the woman's tumour was shown on a screen for the visiting audience to see. Then the doctors began to rapidly chant a sound that means, *'already gone'*, or *'already accomplished'*.

As the audience watched in astonishment while the sounds were chanted, the tumour began to shrink right before their eyes. Amazingly, it disappeared completely in two minutes and forty-two seconds. The story is recounted in Gregg Braden's excellent book, *"The Isaiah Effect."*

Other independent scientists have accurately measured the effects of specific sounds on cancer cells, delivering a specific musical note that destroyed the cells. Other frequencies of sound have been shown to affect viruses and harmful bacteria and even reduce pain.

Maybe there's more truth in the wizardry teachings of Hogwarts than any of us imagine! There might be ancient words, mostly forgotten, that have been used in past times for the most remarkable of things. Who knows? Our understanding of sounds, and how they affect matter - biological and non-biological - is still primitive but deserves a great deal of research.

During 2003 I personally conducted some simple experiments that measured the biological effects of some words.

I wrote the words, *'love'*, *'fear'*, *'happy'*, and *'sad'* on labels and then stuck them to plastic cups. I then put a small amount of water in each of them. By unconsciously triggering tiny levels of emotion in me, I believed that my awareness of each word would imprint energy associated with its meaning, and its sound vibration, into the water in each cup.

I then took a set of thirty pots and put approximately fifty seeds of cress in each of them. I then used the *'love'* labelled cup to water six pots of seeds every day, and I did the same with *'fear'* labelled cups, as well as *'happy'* and *'sad'* labelled cups. I also watered a set of six pots with unlabelled water, to serve as a control.

Each day I put a small, precisely measured, amount of water in each cup and used an exact amount of it to water the seeds.

I used six pots for each word so that I could obtain a statistically accurate result, so that the effect of each word would be measured against three hundred seeds. Each set of six pots received water from the same cup every day so that there was no overlap of words on any seeds. After watering for seven days I individually measured the length of every sprout of cress, something I can assure you was no five-minute task.

The results surprised even me. I discovered that seeds that had been watered from the *'love'* labelled cups grew much taller than seeds watered from the *'fear'* labelled cups, and the seeds watered with *'happy'* water were much taller than seeds grown with *'sad'* water.

There was a 7% difference in the height of sprouts between the *'love'* and *'fear'* cups and a 15% difference between the *'happy'* and *'sad'* ones (*see references*). Happy water made the seeds tallest of all. And this was after only seven days!

Japanese scientist Masaru Emoto went as far as photographing changes in the crystal structure of water brought about by the written word. A year or two earlier than my experiments he had written words, stuck them on bottles of water, and used a technique called Darkfield Microscopy to get photographs of the water after it had been frozen into ice. He showed that different words produced clearly different crystals of ice.

For example, he discovered that the words *'love'*, *'thank you'*, and even *'Mother Theresa'*, produced highly crystalline, sparkly, ice crystals but negative words caused crystals to be dull and undefined. He also recorded differences in the structure of water when different pieces of music were played in the vicinity. Some pieces of classical music, for instance, produced sparkly crystals.

I often write inspiring, compassionate, uplifting, peaceful, or healing words on labels and stick them to bottles of water that I drink from because I believe they will nourish my body in some way.

Before eating anything I also quietly say a few words to myself to acknowledge the fact that I appreciate the food that I am about to eat.

Food for the Soul

Most food contains water so any intentions experienced while preparing it, or prior to eating it, may colour it. Even if it had no water, intentions would still be absorbed by it just as rocks, which are dry, absorb mental and emotional energy, whatever form such energy takes.

Most psychically sensitive people will tell you that buildings still hold the vibrations, or memories, of past times. Scientists even use the fact, in medical science and in electronics, that quartz crystal, which is rock, holds, amplifies, and transmits sound and electromagnetic frequencies, which are also vibrations.

Modern advances in the science of quantum physics have suggested that thoughts are simply faster vibrations of sound than ultrasound, music, or words. To a small degree, music will affect the internal structure of any rocks in the vicinity (like it affects wine glasses), as would ultrasound. So it is logical to assume, then, that thoughts will also be picked up by the internal structure of the rocks at some level

So in some way, any thoughts, feelings, or words expressed around food will colour it to some extent.

Imagine the consequences of three meals a day, three hundred and sixty five days a year, where you said a few words of gratitude as you sat down to eat, or simply just thought them. This might be to the creator or to the people who provided the food for you.

In one year alone that would be one thousand and ninety five times where you might have taken a positive quality of energy into your body as you ate. It would be an interesting scientific study to compare the health of people doing this with people who don't, say, over the course of a year.

In some cultures, food is carefully prepared while being mindful of love and grateful in this way. I find a difference in taste, as well as how I feel afterwards, when I eat food that has been prepared like this.

I attended a talk on food during a meditation retreat in India during 2002, by invitation of the Brahma Kumaris World Spiritual University, and learned how much importance they paid to where it comes from and the way that it is prepared. At the retreat centre, all food is prepared while being mindful of love and is served with a genuine smile and in a spirit of service. I can tell you that the food tasted divine.

There's a lot to be said about taking pride in your cooking. A love of food preparation, cooking, and presentation, may add more to the quality of the meal than you might have imagined.

At one of the lectures, the speaker touched on the subject of vegetarian food. He discussed his opinions of how animal meat might be coloured by the way the animal was treated. An inhumane environment and painful death, for instance, would imprint the animal's fear into the meat. The vibrations of fear would then enter your body as you eat it.

If you are going to eat meat, therefore, it might be better to choose meat that came from animals that had been treated with love and care, or who had roamed free.

It reminded me of something I once heard of how some tribes of Native American Indians would ask the creator to give them food and then, quite frequently, a docile buffalo would wander into their paths almost as if it was offering itself up. It was believed that the animal had naturally come to the end of its lifetime and had made an agreement with the creator, so it felt no fear or pain when it died.

The Indians would thank the creator for the gift of food and thank the buffalo for providing nourishment for the people, genuinely honouring its spirit. Such gratitude and compassion would have undoubtedly coloured the meat with love vibrations, nourishing the bodies of all who ate of it.

I am quite certain that if any scientists wish to analyse some food before and after such feelings were expressed around it, or before and after grace has been said, then they will discover this to be true.

Saying grace, of course, will also affect any water in the vicinity and analysis will also show differences in the way its atoms vibrate.

Holy Water

If an apparition appeared near a stream of water then it would colour the water and the surrounding rocks with the energy emitted from it. It must emit energy, which impacts the rods and cones in the eyes, otherwise it could not be seen.

Some people may believe that apparitions are not real and are merely a figment of the imagination, but I will make an assumption that they are real and that some people just can't see them. As quantum physicists have proven, there are many more forms of energy that can occupy the same space as us, whose vibration is outside of the normal range of perception of the human visual cortex. Every person is unique so there might be some with a slightly larger range than others.

As we have learned, the rocks would absorb the energy just as they absorb any electromagnetic vibrations, heat, or sound. And just as hot rocks slowly give off heat, they would also radiate the energy of the apparition. As water trickled over the rocks it would continue to be coloured by the energy of the apparition.

This might be a reason why holy areas produce healing waters for many years. And its healing qualities may last a very long time because if millions of people know about it, their faith, beliefs, emotions, and intentions will constantly affect it, continually infusing it with healing intentions.

They don't even need to be in the vicinity. Later in the book you will learn how everything in existence is interconnected. A thought of something, or someone, travels there instantly.

A number of scientists have studied our ability to send and receive intentions over great distances. It is called 'Distant Intentional Influence', or more commonly 'Distant Healing'.

6

Distant Healing and Prayer

If a person is in pain or is sick, you help them in some way the instant you wish for her or him to get better. Every intention goes to where it is intended. And research has shown that it doesn't matter whether you are right beside the person or several kilometres away. In fact it wouldn't matter if you were on the moon.

In life the results are seldom obvious because we have conditioned ourselves to believe that a person's recovery is almost always down to medical treatments. Of course, medical intervention has a major effect, but your intentions also make a difference that may be tiny in some instances and larger in others.

If the person gave you permission, you could visualise healing in their body. If they had flu, for instance, you could imagine seeing the virus getting smaller and smaller until it disappeared completely, or you could visualise their body surrounded by a soft healing light. You could even visualise them in perfect health.

Several scientific studies have investigated distant healing, confirming that intention really does affect people over great distances. Typically the experiments have several people in one place visualising, or mentally intending, a change in other people several metres or kilometres away.

In one particular experiment, led by Professor Dean Radin, currently of the Institute of Noetic Sciences in Petaluma, California, but while at the Department of Parapsychology of Edinburgh University, the 'influencers' (the people doing the visualisations or sending mental intentions) were asked to try to either calm or activate the other people (the 'targets'). The experiment involved seven 'influencers' and ten 'targets'.

Over sixteen individual sessions the influencers were able to influence the targets in a room twenty-five metres away. The scientists measured changes in the targets using sensors attached to their skin.

When asked to either calm or activate the targets, the sensors consistently measured a change at the instant the influencers sent their intentions.

Other research has indicated that if they had done the experiment with a few centimetres, or even kilometres, separating the influencers and targets, the results would have been the same. That distance does not matter in matters of the mind!

Several studies have also shown that a person is acutely aware of another person staring at her or him. You have probably noticed this in your own life.

Is it not true that you can often tell when someone is staring at you? Don't you just get a 'feeling'? This is real. Your body is picking up on their thoughts on a biological level and so is your mind. Some people can even physically feel it, which as we already know is probably due to the movement of neuropeptides to specific receptors.

A study, involving ninety-six patients with hypertension, reported that influencers could even reduce the blood pressure of targets. Similarly, this experiment involved influencers in one place and targets in another. Blood pressure measurements, before and after intention was sent, showed a reduction in the blood pressure on account of the intentions of the influencers.

Professor William Braud and co-workers, at the Mind Science Foundation in San Antonio, Texas, also studied blood. They showed that intention could even slow down the bursting of hypertonic (salty) blood cells when the influencers and targets were in separate locations.

An earlier study, published in 1968 by the French physician Jean Barry, even examined effects of intention on fungus. It described the ability of people to mentally control the rate of growth of the fungus.

In the experiment, two 'influencers' conducted nine separate sessions where they used intention to slow down its growth. In 85% of the trials there was a significant reduction in the rate of growth of the fungus.

Distant healers can even alter the growth rate of plants. In one experiment, two healers substantially speeded up the rate of growth of rye grass when they were 500 kilometres away from it.

The grass was monitored as it grew. When the instruction was given for the healers to focus upon it, it immediately started to grow faster. During some periods the rate of growth even increased by over 600%.

In a different kind of study, conducted by William Braud and co-workers, several targets were asked to focus their attention on burning candles. Each time their attention slipped they were to press a button alerting the researchers. And at this instant, an influencer would focus on a burning candle and try to mentally assist some of the targets in their concentration.

The results were significant, showing that the influencers had helped those targets to concentrate.

All of these results clearly imply that anyone can have an effect upon the heart, mind, and body of anyone else. The effects may be very small but sometimes they could be large, so this presents all of us with a moral situation.

A significant degree of responsibility is required to intend no harm towards another. Of course, sometimes it is beneficial to get things out of our systems. Suppressing feelings does no good. But perhaps it is best we do so with as much tact and compassion as possible, for it has been said that we should be careful what we wish for. We should endeavour to forgive, then, and to wish the best for each other, just as you would hope that people wanted the best for you.

Just in case, studies have shown that we can easily block unwanted intentions. It can be as simple as declaring, "*Ever day in every way I am protected from any harmful thoughts, intentions, and emotions of others.*"

In one particular scientific experiment involving thirty-two targets, half of them were asked to shield themselves from the thoughts of the influencers. The researchers found that the targets who wanted to block unwanted intentions could easily do so.

Some practitioners who practise healing techniques are well aware that, during therapy treatments, they pick up their patient's energies - their thoughts, their emotions, and their issues - so they often have to 'psychically protect' themselves.

Some therapists like to visualise wearing a 'cloak of protection' that is made of an imaginary white or golden light that cancels out any harmful thoughts or emotions coming their way.

There is just as much mental and emotional noise surrounding us throughout the day as there is electrical and magnetic 'noise'. Holding a fluorescent bulb underneath an overhead power line will cause it to light up due to the large electromagnetic field radiating from the cables. In a similar way, people are 'lit up' by the mass fields of thoughts and emotions in densely populated areas.

This is why some meditation teachers suggest that we meditate at sunrise or late at night, and is also why some spiritual masters live high in the mountains, or have done their training in such places. Early in the morning or late at night, most people are asleep so there is less mental noise in the air. In a more peaceful air, not crowded with mental and emotional noise, it becomes easier to access a deeper state of meditation.

You may even have noticed, if you climb high hills or mountains, that the air is quieter and more peaceful the higher you climb. The higher you climb, the further away you get from the mental and emotional noise at ground level.

Knowing the effect you have on others, try to be responsible with your intentions towards them. If someone annoys you or has hurt you in the past, try to let it go and forgive them for any wrongdoing. If you do this you won't be putting any harmful 'noise' into the atmosphere. Mark Twain wrote, "*Forgiveness is the fragrance that the violet sheds on the heel that has crushed it.*"

Practising the art of forgiveness can be transformational in your own life. Instead of condemning the actions of another try to feel some compassion for the person. Perhaps they might be in so much inner pain and confusion that they need to act that way. You never know. Instead of seeing a person who's actions you disapprove of, try to see the person underneath who is suffering. Instead of seeking retribution, why not say a prayer for them. As Christ said, *"Forgive them father. For they know not what they do."* Prayers are very powerful because they bring into play faith in the creator as well as intention.

Prayer

One of the best known scientific studies of the power of prayer took place at the University of San Francisco School of Medicine between August 1982 and May 1983. During that time, 393 patients were admitted to the coronary care unit of the hospital and agreed to be involved in the prayer study. It was led by Randolph Byrd MD, and published in the 'Southern Medical Journal' in 1988. Normal medical treatment for all 393 patients took place as required except that approximately half of them were prayed for by a group of Christians who were not in the hospital, and half were not.

The study showed that the overall severity of illness of the patients who were prayed for turned out to be much less than the patients who were not prayed for. The group who were prayed for needed less ventilatory assistance, fewer antibiotics, and fewer diuretics, than the patients who were not prayed for and there was also less need for CPR.

Please note that although Christians participated in this study, prayers from any religious group will be beneficial.

In fact a study took place in 1998 at Duke University Medical Centre where 150 patients underwent heart surgery. Similarly, half of them were prayed for and half were not, but this time by different religious groups.

It was found that the patients who were prayed for had fewer complications and their recovery rates were 50-100% faster than the patients who were not prayed for.

These controlled scientific studies, and many others published in the scientific journals, show that prayer really works. I don't know a single person who hasn't, at some time in their life, called to a Higher Power to make himself, herself, or someone else well, or even to change something in their life. Prayer works, although you might not always see immediate results or results that you intended.

I find that prayer usually brings the 'highest' result, which is the result that is best for me and for everyone else connected with the outcome. The result you get isn't always what you ask for because when you invite God, or whichever deity you pray to, into your life then you are inviting more wisdom and love.

Therefore you will get the wisest, most love-filled, result that is best for everyone. If your intentions are consistent with that, for example if you desire "'this' or something even better that will benefit all concerned", then you will probably get what you pray for or something even better. If not, then the result might be different from what you desire.

You might intend to gain something, for instance, and in your gain someone may lose something. With a prayer you will often notice that if you do gain something then it works out for the best for everyone. The other person will gain too.

And it happens the other way around too. When you genuinely pray for the well-being or success of someone else, you also receive well-being and success. You get back what you send out.

A scientific study in prayer, reported in 1997 in the journal 'Alternative Therapies', found precisely this.

It was led by Fr Seán O'Laoire and reported the effects of prayer on self-esteem, anxiety, and depression. In all, 496 volunteers were involved, 406 as subjects to be prayed for and 90 as agents to do the praying. Three agents prayed for each subject, and prayer was offered daily for 15 minutes for an experimental period of 12 weeks.

Evaluations were made of self-esteem, anxiety, depression, mood, physical health, intellectual health, spiritual health, relationships, and creative expression. In all measures the subjects showed improvement, but the agents also improved in all measures and in some areas - intellectual health, spiritual health, relationships, and creative expression - the improvement was larger than it was for the subjects.

The prayer for the well-being of another enhanced that person's well-being, but also brought well-being to the person offering the prayer for them. You get back what you give out!

Many people use prayer, not only to restore health but also to change aspects of their lives. Ancient Tibetan and Native American

Indian teachings, as well as those in the Dead Sea Scrolls, suggest that there are effective ways to pray and ways that are not so effective. Some of these teachings are described in Gregg Braden's book, *"The Isaiah Effect."*

Such an effective prayer, for instance, is one in which a person begins with a feeling of genuine gratitude for the current situation. Then they imagine what they desire, while speaking to a deity or not, and vividly experience the feelings of their desire being fulfilled. The feeling is key. Lastly, they give thanks for having had the opportunity to choose. You will notice that appreciation and intention, and the associated feelings, are key to an effective prayer formula.

One of the reasons why prayer works, and why visualisation and distant healing work, is because everything in the universe is connected to everything else, as the following chapters describe.

The Nature of Reality

Some modern theories of science, quantum physics to be precise, suggest that everything that exists has condensed out of an all-encompassing 'field' of energy. These theories parallel those of some eastern mystical teachings that talk of all things condensing out of a field of qi or a field of infinite intelligence.

Our scientific theories also suggest that everything in existence is connected to everything else, instantly and intimately in time and space.

Imagine a room full of people and imagine that they are all holding a single piece of rope so that it connects everyone, like a net. Call it an 'inter-net', or a 'web', because it is a net or a web that interconnects everyone.

If someone were to shake one strand of the rope, everyone would feel it because they are all connected by it, just as a spider instantly feels the vibrations of something trapped in its web.

In reality, a vast web connects everyone and everything. You are connected to the forests, the flowers, the weeds, the animals, the insects, the fish, to the mountains and the clouds, and even to the planets and the stars. There are no exceptions. Nothing is left out. No one is alone.

Some scientists believe that the eastern intuitive idea of the nature of reality describes things more accurately than our theories, and perhaps our theories and experiments will eventually confirm this. These teachings tell us that the field of energy is one of conscious intelligence and that everything you see around you is 'frozen' consciousness. They say that consciousness 'con-denses' to form all things in a similar way to how steam condenses to form water. And this description is not too far away from how some modern scientists understand it. Even Albert Einstein believed that matter was merely points in space where the field was very intense, but that the 'quantum field' was the only reality.

The eastern teachings merely extend this to say that the quantum field is alive. And why wouldn't it be? You and I are alive, so any description of reality must take into account that consciousness is present.

So at the most basic level then, all things are composed of consciousness, or at least condensed out of a field of consciousness in the same way that steam condenses into water. Therefore, in the human body, a diseased organ is not an inanimate object but is actually made of consciousness. This is perhaps why it is possible to heal it with visualisation. This may also be why your genes switch on and off according to how you think and feel. Consciousness is affecting consciousness in the same way that steam and water affect ice.

Steam or hot water can be used to sculpt ice. In the same way, thoughts and feelings may sculpt atoms and molecules, restoring health and vitality to any part of the body.

The famous psychologist, Carl Gustav Jung, also wrote about the connection between things. He proposed the idea of a 'collective unconscious', which is a group unconscious mind that connects everyone together.

He wrote that each of us has a conscious mind and an unconscious mind. The conscious part is the day-to-day part of our mind that we think with. We use it intentionally for everyday efforts, like moving our arms and legs, speaking, smiling, singing and dancing, and to alter our breathing.

The unconscious is much larger. Just as you use your conscious mind to move your body, the unconscious mind intentionally moves your cells. It also controls your heartbeat, the workings of your hormones, and even the production and movement of your neuropeptides. Because it is controlling many more things it is usually out of reach of our conscious mind. This is why it is called the unconscious.

Jung proposed that, together, we have a group unconscious mind where each of us is connected through our unconscious minds. Therefore all information about everything is available to everyone, just like vibrations can be felt all over a web. Such unconscious knowledge can be accessed by anyone just as the Internet connects all computers and can be accessed by anyone.

Most people imagine that the Internet is the network of computers, but it is not. Neither is it the cables or servers. It is the information. The computers are merely devices used to access this information. When a new website is uploaded it changes the Internet slightly, not because it affects the computers, but because the total information contained in the Internet is now different.

Similarly, the collective unconscious represents the total information, or intelligence, of all of us. Whenever new thoughts are made, or ideas generated, it is just like a new website has been posted (uploaded). It changes the information and intelligence of all of us.

So a vast interconnecting web, which is part of an all-encompassing field of conscious intelligence, connects us and we share a collective intelligence that is available to anyone. In this way the entire universe vibrates to the tune of the tiniest thought or idea.

This is the underlying reason why knowledge travels so quickly. It rarely waits until it is read or heard, it is intuitively known by everyone as it vibrates along every stand that interconnects us. We may learn things through books, newspapers, or from the TV, but at an unconscious level we knew already. These physical devices, whose creation was unconsciously inspired, merely tell us what is already in our unconscious minds.

In a way, they act like computers connected to the Internet that enables us to download information. We are limited, then, only by our speed of connection. And just as our modern advances are providing better and faster ways of accessing information from the internet, it is merely reflecting that fact that we are evolving in our understanding of consciousness, and so enhancing our abilities to access information from the collective unconscious.

Indeed, looking at the expansion in the number of books published in the mind-body-spirit field, it would appear that more and more people are understanding consciousness and so it is likely that our abilities at accessing unconscious information will also improve. And as it does so you will find that we will discover faster and faster ways to communicate.

And as each new person understands consciousness and our interconnectedness, their ideas further vibrate throughout the web, inspiring similar ideas and intuitions in others. Looking at our changing world, I believe that this knowledge is already inspiring us to feel differently, and therefore to act differently. And the consequences of our feelings and our actions are profoundly affecting the world.

For instance, we intuitively know that the health of the 'web', just like a spider's web, is co-dependent upon every strand. If one strand is broken, the overall health suffers, even though other strands may appear to be strong. Knowing this, we are becoming more responsible in our actions, seeking ways of living that are of mutual benefit to all.

It is not always obvious, but there are growing pockets of change occurring everywhere in the world where ways of working together are being created upon principles of kindness, fairness, peace, unity, honesty, connectedness, and love.

For example a growing number of businesses with visionary leaders, while retaining their goals of continuous growth, also recognise that they are part of a whole. They ensure that their growth benefits the whole; otherwise there is no point. If something is gained at the expense of another, or of any part of nature, then we all lose in the long term. In other words, if one strand of the web gained the material of another strand then a hole is created in the web, it weakens, and the overall health suffers.

In his paradigm shifting book, *"Birth of the Chaordic Age"*, Dee Hock, founder of VISA International, explains how and why some corporations are adapting in this way.

He explains that within some businesses, the leaders and all of their employees have created a shared moral and ethical sense of purpose, and a shared set of principles of conduct of how they commit to treating each other. Common sense will tell you that such corporations and organisations will flourish because everyone shares a similar vision.

Typically, employees of many corporations and organisations don't feel themselves, at a deep level, to be part of such a moral and ethical vision for the betterment of humanity. However, intuitively, they feel they should be. The knowledge that it is possible is vibrating throughout the 'web'. This is why cracks appear in corporations who still operate by the old rules.

In many places stress and employee dissatisfaction have reached epidemic proportions. There is often a huge gulf between the goals and behaviours of the company and the inner sense of purpose and behaviour of its employees. The rules are changing, because people are changing, because what's in the collective unconscious is changing.

The true power of a business, or of an individual, is evolving - from who *has* the most to who *serves* the most. Watch over the next few years as you see this happening.

If you look around you can see more of the changes. For example, investment in ethical businesses is now higher than ever before. There is also a growing desire in the world to respect nature, protecting the environment and endangered species. There is more focus, now, on human rights than ever before in history. More people than ever before will no longer accept the bullying or abuse of another person. They understand that 'it doesn't have to be that way'. There is also a growing movement in 'Fairtrade', paying a fair price for goods and services, particularly in developing countries. Our efforts to charitably help each other are also expanding. People from all over the world race to help their brothers and sisters in need.

On December 26th 2004, a tsunami struck East Asia and caused untold devastation as thousands lost their lives and millions were left homeless. Yet, in a demonstration of global compassion, unrivalled in modern times, the people of the world rallied together to donate money to help the survivors and to help in rebuilding the communities that were destroyed. In my own country I read of children giving up their presents, others selling some of their personal belongings, people were donating money over the telephone and the Internet, and others put their loose change in collection cans in numerous shops and businesses. Musicians, sports people, and entertainers even organised special events in aid of the people affected. Together, we helped repair a deep wound and give others hope in the strength of the human spirit.

The world is growing more loving every day as we grow in our consciousness, recognising our interconnection as members of the same human family.

Such changes are growing in intensity and in numbers and they reflect our intuitive sense of connection to one another.

In medicine, more and more scientists are beginning to realise that our mental and emotional attitudes are linked with disease and that we can participate in the healing process of others and ourselves. The number of healthcare practitioners who integrate both complementary and allopathic medicine is growing fast.

People are seeing the world differently from the way they did only a few years ago, and this is evolving the nature of the decisions they make to ones that are more aligned to the benefit of all of humanity.

And as these changes occur they vibrate the 'web', inspiring similar changes in other people in other parts of the world. It is a cycle and it is affecting all of us in our individual lives. And it happens because everything is connected.

8

Experiments in Connectedness

Measurements of Consciousness

Since everything is connected and everything is condensed out of consciousness, and is therefore made of consciousness because its basic substance is such, your thoughts can affect anything. Not just your biology, as we've learned, but even events in your personal life and in the world.

Everything is condensed out of consciousness, and that means the trees, the roads, the buildings, the cars, the animals, the clouds, and the people. Events of your life and in the world are merely a product of the *interaction* of things, and their meaning is a product of your thoughts *about* the interaction.

Therefore there is no event that cannot be influenced by your thoughts.

Most thoughts produce minor vibrations on the 'web' and these thoughts result in minor changes around you, and in the world. Such changes are, however, seldom noticeable unless you are consciously aware of your role in creating your own personal reality. Usually it takes lots and lots of the same kind of thought to have any kind of noticeable effect.

Some scientists have studied this using 'Random Event Generators'. A computer that constantly prints out random numbers is such a thing.

Such numbers should always be random. That's their nature. If you were to show the randomness on a computer screen you would see a straight line that never changes. However, under certain conditions, some scientists have discovered that it does change.

These conditions are when a large number of people are focusing upon the same thing at the same time. Although smaller changes are often observed with just one person, and I have discovered this in my own experiments.

Each thought sends ripples (waves / vibrations) throughout the interconnected universe, just like dropping a pebble in a pond sends ripples outwards.

A single thought from a person produces a small vibration throughout the 'web' that is hardly noticeable in the world, or on the generators, but millions of the same ones cause a big vibration, or tidal wave, like the effect of dropping a huge boulder in a pond. Each identical wave adds to another, 'resonating' with it, causing a multiplication of intensity of the wave. This is noticeable.

Say ten million people heard something on the TV news at the same time and all of them thought, "Whoa!". That would be ten million people whose minds stopped processing a hundred other things and, just for that instant, were focused on the same thing. You would expect this to produce big vibrations. Indeed, numerous experiments have shown that when this type of focusing takes place, a blip appears on the line of the random event generator. It affects the random numbers of the generator.

And such is the force of the focusing of millions of thoughts at the same time it causes a focusing of other things as the entire 'web' is affected. Just as the tidal wave affects everything in its path, lots of the same kind of thought produces a large wave that is easily seen. Events in the world can be seen to be affected.

Imagine if hundreds or even thousands of people focused on 'Peace' at the same time. The force of the thoughts would ripple outwards, affecting many things. Experiments have actually shown this. A few hundred people meditating in one place at the same time, for instance, has affected local crime rates.

The peaceful thoughts vibrate outwards affecting the consciousness of other people nearby, just like the wave produced by dropping a pebble in a small pond will affect everything floating on the surface of the pond, or how vibrations from a struggling fly are felt all over a spider's web.

If it were millions of people focusing upon 'Peace', other people all over the world might find themselves inspired to behave more peacefully towards each other as the large waves power outwards. People going about their daily business may just feel different, unaware of why they feel so good. Others might find problems resolved, since many of our daily difficulties are products of our chaotic minds.

In a 'wave' of inspiration vibrating around the 'web', negotiators in conflict situations might suddenly see the solutions to long-running stand-offs as the know-how suddenly becomes clear in their minds. And both sides of some conflicts might suddenly feel less hostile towards each other and even see less meaning in the fighting than they did previously.

All it takes is for millions of people to focus on 'Peace' at the same time on a regular basis to create a large multiplication of intensity, or resonance effect, of the peaceful thought. With a 'Peace budget' as large as a typical corporate advertising budget, visionary leaders could do a lot of good through the media.

Imagine seeing the words PEACE, LOVE, or HAPPY a hundred or so times throughout your daily newspaper, or hearing those words regularly on the TV news. Or imagine, instead of mostly seeing full-page advertisements selling products, there was the occasional advertisement suggesting that we be kind to each other today.

Seeing the words 'Peace', 'Love', or 'Happy' inspires peace, love, and happiness just as seeing violent words and images inspires violence. As more people hear about, or read about, peace, love, or happiness on a regular basis, the bigger the wave so the larger the effect.

In 2000, some friends and I founded an organisation called 'Spirit Aid'. Our original intention was to organise a special event that would inspire more peace, love, and kindness in the world. We hoped that a large mass of people simultaneously focusing upon such values might inspire positive changes all over the world.

The plan was to hold a concert in a football stadium and beam it live on TV all over the world. And the key was that in-between musical sets we wanted authors and teachers speaking about peace, love, and kindness. We hoped that the combination of music and messages might produce miracles. During the organising phase the nature of the event changed, evolving into a 9-day, 24-event festival of peace in July 2002 that sent waves of peace, love, and kindness around the world.

Similarly, in 2003, the authors and teachers, James Twyman, Gregg Braden, and Doreen Virtue, organised a peace meditation where a few million people around the world 'prayed peace' at exactly the same time, synchronised throughout many different time zones, and it had a powerfully peaceful effect on a conflicting world event at that time. These results, and those involving similar meditations orchestrated by the same people, have been documented.

Individually and collectively we affect each other, and everything in existence, 24 hours a day, 365 days a year through the vibrations we send into the 'web', through the 'websites' we upload that represent the quality of people we are being.

Love inspires more love, whether it is through intentions or actions. Peace inspires more peace, whether it is through intentions or actions. And kindness inspires more kindness, whether it is through intentions or actions. Through our intentions and actions we change the world. We cannot do anything else. The direction of that change is therefore up to us!

ESP

It is not only random event generators that show how things are connected. Modern day multi million dollar particle accelerators demonstrate the interconnectedness of tiny subatomic particles over large distances. A pair of subatomic particles can be sent at fantastic speeds in opposite directions. One of them is then probed and the other instantly feels it. Numerous simple ESP (Extra Sensory Perception) experiments also show it.

A typical ESP experiment is where a person has to guess which of several cards is being held up. The picture on the card might be a circle, a square, a triangle, or wavy lines, and the person has to guess which. Research has shown, beyond any shadow of a doubt, that 'guessers' are aware of which card is being held up.

In 1994, a psychologist named Julie Milton, at the University of Edinburgh in Scotland, collected and summarised the results of seventy eight individual scientific studies involving ESP guesses by 1,158 ordinary people, that had been published in the scientific journals between 1964 and 1993.

Her analysis concluded, with odds against achieving the results by chance of over ten million to one, that ESP was real.

If you think about it, in a typical experiment the person guessing and the person holding up the card being guessed are connected, and so also are the person guessing and the card being guessed. The people and the cards are made of the same stuff and are part of the 'web'.

Therefore the identity of the card (its unique type of vibration) is available to the guesser, at least on an unconscious level. All that is required is for the information to be 'downloaded' from the 'web' into the personal conscious mind of the guesser, just as information is downloaded from the Internet onto our personal computers.

To someone skilled at downloading it is just as if the card is being held up with its picture in full view. As you might expect, there are people very skilled at downloading. Some psychics are adept at it.

If we could learn to tap into the collective unconscious mind at will, improving our download connection speed, then we would gain some of its knowledge and wisdom. You would, therefore, expect hypnosis to improve ESP ability because it is known to access the unconscious mind.

In 1994, scientists at the University of New York investigated this. They analysed the results of 25 scientific studies that had been published in scientific journals between 1945 and 1982 and indeed discovered that hypnosis improved people's ability to perform well in ESP studies.

ESP and psychic ability is natural. It is only our beliefs that they are not possible that obstruct our abilities. But anyone can practise ESP or become more psychic. Sometimes in the evening, while I was a university student, I tried to train myself. At first, without practise, I could guess the colour of the next card in a randomly shuffled deck of cards maybe four or five times at best, which you would expect to be normal. But through practise, which involved learning to recognise intuitions, I was able to score consistently higher and once, with much meditation practise (almost self-hypnosis), I guessed the colour of the card eleven times in a row and with five of the cards I even guessed the suit. I just had a 'feeling' about each card.

I am no more gifted than anyone else. Anyone can learn to tap into the unconscious, just as anyone can learn to connect her or himself to the Internet. In fact we tap into the collective unconscious all the time.

There is a constant flow of information between the collective unconscious mind and your daily awareness, as you feel every vibration, even though most of the time you are not aware of where specific thoughts, intuitions, and impulses come from. In the same way, a leaf floating on the surface of a pond feels the waves created by different pebbles dropped into the pond in various places but is unaware of the source of each wave.

In our daily lives we are often faced with decisions and frequently make a choice based upon what feels most right. It may be that we feel vibrations regarding the probable outcome of each choice, the knowledge of which is present in the collective unconscious, and so we make the choice that we feel is right for us.

Many people believe that angels and spirit guides watch over them and help them with life's challenges. Some native cultures share such beliefs and, according to numerous surveys, so too does a very large portion of western culture. When I give talks, a quick show of hands often reveals that over 90% of the audiences share these beliefs.

If you assume that angels and spirit guides exist then they must be part of the 'web' since there cannot be anything separate from the web. We are conscious beings and in a universe with consciousness as its most basic building block it is quite likely that intelligence takes forms other than what we recognise as human. Therefore it seems quite probable that, as intelligent entities, they could 'download' information to us concerning the best course of action to take when we are faced with a choice. Many people claim to have been so inspired.

I had an amazing experience in late 2002. I had created a website for Spirit Aid but I had then moved on to other things (including writing this book). My late friend, Pat, was taking over responsibility for the website and asked if I could give her a disc with the website on it.

I didn't have any CDs to save it onto so I went to the shops to buy some. When I was there I noticed several packs of floppy discs and I felt a sudden impulse that I should buy them and save the website onto floppy discs instead of CD's. But I ignored the feeling and bought a pack of CD's because they have larger storage capacity.

When I arrived home I opened up the website files on my computer, put a CD in the CD drive and pressed 'Save'. But it didn't work. I tried again and again but I couldn't get the website to save onto the CD. I tried every CD in the pack but had no success and began to assume that they were damaged in some way. I had agreed to hand the website to Pat the next morning so I was beginning to feel a wee bit concerned that I wouldn't have it ready on time. Knowing that such a mindset wouldn't help, I got up and decided to leave it until later when I might feel more relaxed.

Since it was a nice day my partner, Elizabeth, and I went for a drive. We had no idea where we wanted to go so just kept on driving. Each time we passed an exit from the motorway we wondered if we should take it but always decided that we should drive on. Turning off the motorway at those times didn't feel right. Eventually I picked up the map to see if I felt inspired to visit any place in particular. I noticed a small village on the River Forth that I had never heard of before so I suggested that we should go there.

We arrived after having driven for almost an hour and pulled into an empty car park on the outskirts of the village. It was like a ghost town, and I quite expected to see tumbleweeds roll past. But as we pulled up to park our car, our attention was drawn to something odd. There was a small box lying on the ground, in one of the empty designated parking spaces.

I looked at it and, to my shock, discovered that it was a box of floppy discs. I couldn't believe it. We were in the middle of nowhere, tumbleweeds rolling by, in an empty car park, in a place that we picked from the map, and we found a box of floppy discs.

I decided not to touch them in case someone had dropped them, hadn't realised, and were now on their way back to collect them. Although judging by the lack of life anywhere to be seen, I thought maybe this was unlikely. But we left them alone anyway.

We walked around the village, had some lunch, and returned a couple of hours later, only to discover that the discs were still there, not surprisingly as we had only seen about half a dozen people all day, including two who worked in the café where we had lunch. They were still in the place where we found them. By now I was getting the message. They must be meant for me, so I took them.

When we got home, and after dinner, I decided to have another go at saving the website onto CD. I made a few more attempts before the penny finally dropped. I was trying to save a file onto a CD when I didn't even have a CD-Writer. I was trying to do it from the normal CD ROM drive (I had an old computer).

For the last year, among my other responsibilities, I had been the designated IT person in the charity office and had troubleshooted about every conceivable computer problem and software usage that you can image. This, and I didn't even realise that I needed a CD-Writer to save files onto CD. I had needed floppy discs all along.

It was a very large website, and as I was saving the files the computer kept telling me that each successive disc had become full. When the website was finally saved it had taken all ten floppy discs from the box, with absolutely no space left over at the end. I just looked up and said, "Thanks!"

So coming back to ESP, people receive information from the collective unconscious mind all the time because it is not possible to disconnect from it. It seems that the more relaxed and mentally uncluttered we are, the clearer is the information that we receive. The technique I used in my personal ESP experiments firstly helped me to relax, clearing some of the mental noise that often obstructs connection. But it also helped me to overcome some residual beliefs that I held at the time that ESP wasn't possible, and so caused me to have more faith that it was possible.

And this, I discovered after several more experiments, was the key to my ability. Like a placebo effect, my belief made it easier for me to access information. Faith, I discovered, meant the difference between 'broadband' (or DSL) and 'dial up'.

A belief that it is not possible seems to obstruct the 'connection' and therefore the flow of information from the unconscious to the conscious. This is why people who are sceptical don't get good results.

A lot of people can be sceptical as to whether anything out of their mind-set is possible, and you have probably heard them say, "*I'll believe it when I see it.*" But people who have accomplished great things in life will testify to it being the other way around. Ability follows belief. As author Dr Wayne Dyer aptly titled one of his books, "*You'll see it when you believe it.*"

Sheep and Goats

In 1993, a psychologist named Tony Lawrence, at the University of Edinburgh in Scotland, gathered together the results of 685,000 ESP guesses by 4,500 people, performed over a 50-year period from 1943 until 1993. They were called sheep-goat experiments.

A sheep-goat experiment is one that compares the ESP abilities of people who believe that it is possible, against people who do not.

He published his analysis of them, showing that believers (sheep) were much better at ESP than non-believers (goats). And the odds against achieving such results by chance were a staggering one trillion to 1.

People who believe in ESP are better at ESP than people who don't. The placebo effect extends much further than taking empty pills. People who don't believe in ESP obstruct their own connection.

People who are open to believe that everything is connected give themselves the ability to gain great wisdom and understanding of life through enhancing their 'connection'. And one of the by-products I have noticed is that they also tend to find meaning in their own lives and begin to recognise the contribution that their presence makes to the world.

Belief is a powerful thing. Imagine if we are willing to believe that the world is a good place, populated by billions of kind and compassionate people. We might collectively inspire more kindness and compassion in the world through the waves we create. As more of us begin to see the world in this way, focusing upon the goodness, our thoughts resonate with each other and multiply the power of the wave.

In the same way a cynical view, focusing instead upon the smaller numbers of people who sometimes act differently, might inspire unhappiness. But there's always what can be viewed as positive and negative in the world.

Its how you choose to look at it that determines what you get most of. We don't all need to try to change the world. All you really need to do is change your mind *about* the world. You will come to see that it is a beautiful place, with beautiful people, and if you are willing to believe in the beauty that you see then your faith will move mountains!

9

Who Am I?

Consciousness condenses to form physical things analogously to the way that steam condenses to form water and ice. Everything is created in this way, making consciousness the basic building block of the entire universe. This idea has been held in mystical teachings for millennia, and in the last century a similar idea has been embraced by a number of scientists.

Indeed, there are some parallels between mystical teachings, which are based upon spiritual experience, and modern science, which is based upon intuition and reasoning.

Some mystical teachings tell us that it is a single consciousness that is the building block, or source, and that it is infinitely intelligent. This consciousness is often referred to as God and thus all things are parts of God.

In quantum physics, it is believed that all matter comes from the quantum field and that all things are different expressions of the field.

Thus, there is a striking similarity between both ideas. Mystics hold that all matter condenses from the field of infinite intelligence and quantum physics holds that all matter appears at points where the quantum field is most intense. Since we are conscious beings, I believe that an accurate description of reality must include consciousness therefore I resonate with the mystical teachings, while also embracing the theories of quantum physics, since both understandings merely seem to look at the same thing in different ways.

So if all things have their source in the field of infinite intelligence it might then be assumed that there are no accidents and that every form is created, therefore, to appear just as it is supposed to appear and to perform exactly as it does.

Somehow in the process of condensation we lose awareness of our true nature. It is like a droplet condensing out of an ocean of conscious intelligence and in noticing that it has become a droplet it forgets that it was once, and is still, part of the ocean. You might liken it to an iceberg floating upon the surface of the ocean. Our conscious awareness represents the tip of the iceberg, but the greater part of us - call it the *Higher Self* - is beneath the surface.

We thus learn to define ourselves purely in terms of our physical form. We believe ourselves to be purely our physical bodies, since all we see is the tip of the iceberg, and we assume that our consciousness is merely the product of the interaction of different chemicals in the brain. However, just as the tip of the iceberg is connected to the main body, regardless of whether it is aware of it or not, we are connected to our Higher Selves regardless of whether we are aware of it or not. It does, however, seem that deep within all of us is a degree of instinctual awareness of our true nature since we cannot be disentangled from it.

Some teachers hold that our purpose in life, then, is to regain total awareness of this and we call this state of regaining full awareness, enlightenment.

How we experience each situation in life reflects our degree of enlightenment. An unenlightened person might see the loss of a personal possession, for instance, precisely as a loss and possibly assume that it is the result of a theft, but an enlightened person might see the same situation as part of a cosmic energy pattern unfolding and experience it as a blessing, or perhaps he or she might be so unconcerned that they might not even notice. Life, then, is a journey of experiences leading us to enlightenment.

Each experience provides us with yet another opportunity to realise our true nature - that we are *'in this world but not of this world'*. Our form may change with time and things may happen to us, but we are eternal and are walking a path towards realising that we *are* the infinite intelligence, simply suffering from a little amnesia.

Our temporary state of amnesia, not remembering that we are the creator, is why we appear to lack the abilities to heal ourselves of any illness or to make positive changes in our lives. It is a cosmic placebo effect.

Our deep belief in who we think we are causes us to perform in accordance with what limits we believe in. But we do not lack any of these abilities. They are latent within us, just as the real power of the iceberg lies beneath the surface.

Such abilities are probably even 'encoded' in our DNA as sets of genes just as the ability to run fast is encoded as genes. Thus, our beliefs affect whether such genes are on or off just as a belief in athletic ability, for instance, will usually make a person a better athlete. At present, these 'healing' or 'transformational' genes are switched off in most people. But it is likely that such genes merely await our genuine recognition of who we really are, at which time they may switch on.

Since each of us condensed from infinite intelligence, and that this intelligence is our true nature, and that there can be no accidents in the universe, we personally created the atoms that formed our bodies, only we don't remember. In fact we are personally creating our bodies right now.

Every cell in your body is continually being re-created, as old cells die and new ones are born. In this way, the entire body is constantly being renewed under your direction.

Clearly this is not conscious. The part of us that is doing this represents the main body of the iceberg – the Higher Self. If the conscious mind is the mind that we use to move our bodies, then the unconscious mind is the mind that our Higher Self uses to create atoms and molecules. So the creation of our bodies is unconscious in us.

Your Higher Self intended to create your body just the way it is, then, otherwise it would not exist. The intention to create it would have produced ripples throughout the web (field / infinite intelligence / ocean of consciousness), just as a stone would produce ripples if it were dropped on still water. The idea of what your body should look like was the blueprint that probably condensed as sets of genes in your DNA.

Just as there is a point where steam starts to condense to form droplets of water, there must exist a point where vibrations, or waves, of consciousness start to condense to form subatomic particles (the tiny particles that atoms are made of). Each Higher Self probably shapes the way the particles combine, just as a sculptor shapes his creations, so that atoms, proteins, enzymes, and DNA are created exactly as was intended, according to the blueprint. Perhaps the intention, or blueprint, is the underlying predisposition behind the switching on of certain genes.

So the DNA might be much more than an inherited genetic code, it probably codes the intention of the Higher Self. As genes are expressed through life, that intention becomes materialised as the physical body.

As we know, however, through our daily thoughts we influence some of our genes so we are never stuck with a decision made unconsciously by ourselves. We have the freedom of free will to make any changes that we choose to make, in accordance with what we believe is possible of course. Our intentions can be very powerful and affect the actual creation of matter.

Our intentions, and their associated visualisations and emotions, presumably influence the point at which consciousness condenses into particles.

Say you wanted to visualise the healing of a damaged organ. The organ, like the entire body, is constantly being regenerated. When you make new healthy images through visualisation you influence the creation process, sending images to the place and moment when vibrations become particles, and so influencing the nature of the particles. In this way, many new cells are born according to the healthy images (the blueprint) you modelled them upon. The more you visualise, the more new healthy cells are created like this. This is why visualisation is known to have produced seeming miracles.

Where a damaged organ remains damaged for several weeks, new cells have completely replaced old ones. Yet the new ones have adopted a damaged state. Why? Perhaps because you believed it was damaged. Like a placebo effect this belief, and the mental images and feelings associated with it, influenced the creation of new cells so that they became perfect copies of the old ones.

However, it is not as if we are easily able to switch off a belief in illness. Such beliefs are very powerful because the reality of illnesses is part of daily life for many people and, therefore, is a very deeply ingrained worldwide belief. To create such miracles requires an ability to overturn, or transcend, this powerful belief and, as such, there are few people on the planet who have demonstrated the ability; otherwise there would be no such thing as illness. But that does not mean that it is not possible for anyone.

We all have the capacity to overturn beliefs in disease and to form healthy beliefs, because our current state of beliefs is just the tip of the iceberg. And in the end, it's the strongest belief that wins. If a belief in health is stronger than the belief in illness then the illness will disappear, and vice versa.

Through the interconnectedness of all things, we create the reality of our lives by the same process. In fact our lives usually quite accurately reflect the state of our minds. So our conscious thoughts, emotions, and our beliefs have a powerful effect upon the events that seem to happen to us.

Have you ever noticed that when you hurry to reach someplace at a specific time that obstacles almost always appear in your path? If you are driving you can bet that a slow driver will be ahead of you, or others will cut in front of you. You might even stumble into a traffic jam.

In your home or office you will usually fumble some stuff, maybe even drop a pile of papers, or the lid off a bottle you are using and it will miraculously discover an unknown corner of the room, escaping you as you search for it.

The belief that you are late causes you to hurry, but it also causes things like these to happen. Life mirrors our beliefs so that events happen that simply agree with them.

I remember once when I was running very late for an appointment. I was hurrying and began to notice a series of obstacles appearing as I drove. Most of us, when such obstacles arise, hurry even more, but this just creates more obstacles. We even start to curse the obstacles. And, believe me, I have done this on more than one occasion of my life. However, after years of repeating the same thing I began to realise that what is required during such times is the opposite.

On this occasion I decided to do, in fact, the opposite. Instead of hurrying even more I chose to pull over and spend a few moments relaxing. While hurrying I was reinforcing a belief that said, "*I am late.*" By pulling over, a new belief was forming in my mind. Even though I was consciously aware of my lateness, my actions were contradicting this and thus removing the very foundations of the belief. A new unconscious belief was beginning to form, which was a result of my pulling over, that said, "*I have plenty of time.*" Unconscious beliefs often form according to our actions.

After about five minutes of relaxation I started up the car again and peacefully drove to my destination. When I arrived it turned out that my host was also running late and my 'lateness' had, thankfully, given her more time to get ready.

By changing my actions and my belief I changed what was happening. I avoided obstacles that had potential to cross my path and I gave my host all the time she needed to organise herself.

Changing any area of your life is well within your control and you need never be at the mercy of any person, organisation, or situation. Changing your life is the product of changing your mind – your thoughts, your emotions, and what you believe. Visualising how you want things to be is a good way to change anything and huge numbers of people have found this to be successful.

Although I have noticed that while most people have a degree of immediate success in making life changes this way, things often eventually revert back to the way they were before or they eventually find themselves in a similar situation. This is because, while visualisation and intentions are powerful enough to make obvious changes, your old beliefs often reassert themselves. As they do, negative things just 'seem to happen'. But such happenings are merely a product of your old beliefs that did not change significantly enough when you created your new reality.

For instance, say you found yourself in a job you didn't like and you longed for something better. You might start to visualise your 'new job' and quite shortly, as if my magic, you would get an interview and be offered a job that turned out to be very close to what you imagined. This is natural and simply demonstrates the nature of creation.

For a few weeks all might be great in your life but, soon, changes begin to occur in the new workplace. Some people move on and new people join. Some internal systems and practises change. You start to have disagreements with some of your new workmates. And before long you find yourself in a similar situation, perhaps even worse, to the one you left.

This is usually because while you were in the old job you built up a few unconscious beliefs, invisible to you, like '*I don't deserve a meaningful job*' or '*I can't get a good job*', or '*Its not possible to be in a meaningful job*', or '*people are not nice*', or some other relevant belief. These beliefs built up because you interpreted your experience in work, often unconsciously, in one of these ways.

For example, if I had little or no success in getting a new job, despite sending out a large number of applications, I might build up a belief that '*I can't get a good job*'. Each rejected application reinforces the belief and therefore makes it even more difficult to get a job.

As you do this in your own life, powerful beliefs begin to build that ensure that your experience of work remains 'according to your beliefs'. Thus you create a reality in accordance with your thoughts, emotions, and what you believe.

This has happened to me on a number of occasions but I have found that there are a few ways to make lasting changes.

The first requires courage and is to take big actions, significant enough that there is no turning back. Therefore there is little possibility of your old beliefs recreating a similar situation because things have changed so much that it is almost impossible to believe the way you did before. For example, the belief that you are stuck in a job you hate will certainly change if you resign.

The second is more subtle, but immensely powerful in making lasting changes, and is to examine your attitudes and beliefs about yourself, your life, and the world.

For instance, you might write down how you feel. Cover several pages if you need to, listing all your grievances, annoyances, judgements, frustrations, and things from the past. But do so with the thought that there is a belief, or a few beliefs, that are causing things to be the way they are and that you intend to discover it. There are lots of books that can show you how to do this.

Do this, identify the root belief and change it by writing down its opposite, and then visualise what you choose. You will now often find that when things change in your life the change is lasting.

The power of belief is immense. We know how powerful the placebo effect is in creating health but, as you can see, a similar type of placebo effect happens in our daily lives and influences what happens to us. Our thoughts and feelings not only affect our bodies, they affect our lives.

Beliefs make vibrations of thoughts and intentions much bigger. The more faith you have, the bigger the vibrations! Since vibrations of consciousness are the basic building block of everything, beliefs and faith have a profound effect on your body and on your life.

Looking closer, I have found that if I examine the nature of a belief in something I find that the belief is merely a feeling of certainty. I believe, then, that it is not so much the belief but the feeling *produced* by the belief that is important. It carries the power.

'Feelingisation'

Looking at the placebo effect from my own experience, I recognise that feelings carry great power. If a person with a headache takes a placebo, believing it to be a painkiller, then the pain will most likely go away. The belief that the medicine was a painkiller was the healing factor, but I believe that within the belief it was the feeling that was the ultimate cure. The belief created a feeling of certainty that the pain would go away. This is why you can have a strong belief or a weak belief. A strong belief is a strong feeling of certainty while a weak belief is a weak feeling of certainty.

When a person feels 'moved' to tears, it is the feeling that produces the tears. It is not so much the event, but the feelings *produced* that have biological consequences. The feeling causes biological changes that result in tears.

Going even deeper, the creation of proteins in the body is a product of feeling during the memory storage process. Scientific studies have suggested, as we learned in chapter 3, that strong feelings accompanying an experience will ensure that it is encoded strongly as proteins. Each mental and emotional replay of the event re-expresses the genes that manufacture the proteins in the brain. It is the feeling that leads to re-expression of the genes.

In a real sense, then, feelings create matter in this way. They influence the condensation process. So perhaps the best way to visualise good health is to generate a *feeling* of good health while you visualise. Similarly, the best way to create life changes is to generate a feeling of what the new reality would be like. I call this

'Feelingisation', instead of visualisation, to emphasise the need to feel. The mental image merely gives direction to the feeling.

Using the new job analogy, you might then imagine yourself in the new job while vividly feeling the emotions of what it would be like. The feeling carries the creative power.

Any thoughts, then, which carry a strong emotional charge will be quickly materialised, and those without any feeling will take longer to become reality. And this means both positive and negative thoughts.

Positive thoughts charged with strong emotion will swiftly become your reality, but negative ones also accompanied with strong emotion stand the same chance. However, any negative experience so created can be just as quickly neutralised with a surge of positive thought and emotion.

So all thoughts can be amplified by the power of feeling or belief (faith), which is merely a feeling of certainty.

When you have a lot of faith, therefore a great feeling of certainty, healing in the body or life changes can be instantaneous. This is why the placebo effect heals. When you take a dummy medicine, or are given a suggestion, you believe you will recover and so have a feeling of certainty. The amplified power of the thought that you will recover is able to influence the creation process, where vibrations condense into particle droplets. And it does so to a degree according to your level of belief. When you believe (feel certain) you will recover instantly then you do. When you believe (feel certain) it will take time then it takes time.

The degree to which you believe (feel certain), then, governs the rate at which you are healed, or at which your life changes. As

Christ said, "*Do you believe that I am able to do this? They say to him, Yea, Lord. Then he touched their eyes, saying, **According to your faith, be it unto you**. And their eyes were opened.*" **Mathew 9:28**.

Faith, then, is much more than 'mind over matter'. It is really 'mind creates matter'.

When you fully move beyond your amnesia, creation can be instantaneous. From a higher state of consciousness you no longer just believe that you create your body and your life, you *know* (which is a feeling of total certainty). To the Higher Self, creation is instantaneous.

Spiritual teachings tells us that it is possible for us to grow enough in our consciousness in the direction of the Higher Self, revealing more of the iceberg, so that we gain some of the knowing of the Higher Self, at which point nothing is impossible. At such a level of consciousness, beliefs (and so feelings of certainty) about what is possible are intense.

Indeed, Christ said: "*I tell you the truth, if anyone says to this mountain, 'Go, throw yourself into the sea,' and does not doubt in his heart but believes that what he says will happen, it will be done for him. Therefore I tell you, whatever you ask for in prayer, believe that you have received it, and it will be yours.*" **Mark 11: 22-24**.

You will be aware that Christ and Krishna could materialise solid objects out of thin air, turn water into wine, and perform instant healings. Their knowing was so great that they could consciously condense vibrations into particles, commanding the formation of atoms and molecules out of thin air. Much more of their iceberg was revealed and so they lived as if they were Higher Selves.

Years of meditation and practising enlightened attitudes and behaviours, exercises that can develop consciousness, are known to give yogis and mystics more conscious control over the creation process and this is why they are able to perform many miraculous feats.

Such feats are becoming more and more possible in a growing number of people because the knowledge of our true nature is vibrating through the web, inspiring more and more people. Consequently, more and more people every day are recognising the interconnectedness and one-ness of all things. In my own life, I have observed this more and more with each passing year.

People whom you might never have imagined would do so are now thinking about healing, spiritual connections, angels, and the effects of thoughts and emotions on the body, and embracing such ideas as if they had thought that way all their life.

I have spoken with people from different parts of the world who agree that the same is happening where they live too.

Collectively, our attitudes and behaviours are changing and so we are changing the world. Not only do we affect our bodies but all of us, together, collectively send thoughts, intentions, and feelings to the moments of creation, where vibrations condense into particles, and constantly shape the nature of events in the world. Just as our personal thoughts influence biological events in our bodies and events of our lives, our collective thoughts generate tidal waves that influence world events.

So as we are evolving in our consciousness, moving beyond our temporary state of amnesia, we are changing the world. It is becoming more beautiful every day because we are making it so.

At times it may not appear to be so, but events that are not obvious examples of love are simply 'healing in progress'. Sometimes to jump high you need to dip first to generate the momentum. Perhaps the same happens in our lives and in the world at large.

Love is our natural state so is being revealed everywhere as we evolve in our consciousness. It was behind the intention of the Higher Self to create your body and it was behind God's intention to form the entire universe.

Love

Love is the force behind all intentions. It is the essence behind the intentions that form vibrations that later condense to form particles. If blowing on still water is the creative force that makes waves on water, then love is the substance of the wind that forms the waves which organise themselves into atoms and molecules, which themselves form the human body and all things in existence.

That is why it is said that God breathed life into the universe. Every working part of your body was created, with love, out of thin air and ultimately has God as the intelligence behind its shape, its form, and what it does. And as you are ultimately this intelligence, even though it might not yet be conscious in you, you are the guiding intelligence behind all things. What a responsibility!

It has been said that if you act wealthy you will become wealthy, or if you act poor you will become poor. If you consistently ask yourself, when faced with challenging situations, *"What would God do now?"* and act according to the answer you get, then you will evolve in your consciousness. And through this you will make a more consciously positive difference in the world.

Every action you take in life is ultimately motivated by love even though experiences often cloud our judgements, leading us to act in ways that appear quite far removed from love. This state, the absence of love, is the state of total amnesia called fear.

Love and fear are the roots of all experience.

10
Love, Fear, and Biology

Love has a powerful effect on the body, naturally, because it is the force behind its creation. Common sense would therefore tell you that a heart and mind full of love will give you more success in healing yourselves, others, your plants, your pets, your life, and even the world.

A scientific study at Ohio State University of Medicine was examining the effects of a high fat and high cholesterol diet on rabbits. Scientists were feeding them the diet for a period of time then examining them for evidence of atherosclerosis. The atherosclerosis level was expected to be very high throughout the rabbits but one group had 60% less of it than the other groups. Eventually it was discovered that one of the technicians had taken this group out of their cages every day and stroked them. A repeat of the experiment confirmed this. The loving action of care and compassion had reduced levels of atherosclerosis by 60%.

It had altered the biology of the rabbits enough to give them some protection from the damaging effects of a high fat and cholesterol diet.

This came as an initial surprise to the researchers, but it should come as no surprise to you given what you have learned so far in this book; like the fact that depriving an infant of a mother's loving touch affects its genes. Stroking of the rabbits no doubt caused an increase in gene expression that brought about protection from disease.

Love also helps the growth of children. A child growing up in a positive, love-filled, environment may grow larger, denser, prefrontal lobes, containing more communication connections to other parts of the brain. The feeling of love aids the biology-building process.

Love is also important in successful prayer. When you pray for someone's health or well-being, a good prayer contains a feeling of care and compassion for the person you pray for. And God, or whatever deity you pray to, is unconditionally loving so the love is coming from two directions with prayer.

Love is important in all forms of healing. People who practise healing techniques know that the starting point is always love (care, compassion, and a genuine willingness to help).

In the example of the cacti giving up their thorns, love and tenderness was key. I am sure that you will agree with the old tale that talking to your plants makes them grow better. There is real truth here, especially if you speak kindly to them.

In my own plant research described earlier, the words 'love' and 'happy' caused cress seeds to grow much faster than normal. Seeds, like all life, thrive in a positive and loving environment.

You can easily conduct your own simple experiments to confirm this by measuring the growth of your plants over a couple of weeks, either with a ruler or by taking photographs. Talk to them kindly every day and you will find that they will respond to your kindness, just as people do. They will grow taller, stronger, and be healthier.

Fear, as you would expect, has the opposite effect on biology. In my own research, the words 'fear' and 'sad', for instance, suppressed the growth of the seeds of cress. You may also have noticed that plants do not generally grow as well in negative or depressive environments.

Consistent anger and frustration, both qualities of fear, can suppress the immune system in people and make their heart rhythms shaky. Appreciation, care, and compassion, which are qualities of love, do the opposite. Fear is destructive to health, whereas love is constructive.

We also know that sustained neglect of an infant, which probably leaves it feeling alone and fearful, suppresses specific genes so much that its growth is hampered. Loving touch and attention increases gene expression, forming more growth hormones that increase growth of the child.

In general, love promotes health and growth of mind, body, and spirit, whereas fear has the opposite effect.

Love and Intention

Any form of healing starts with love. Healing means to 'make whole'. Love always seeks to make whole. Visualisation works better when love is first felt because the feeling carries the power. In some distant healing plant growth experiments, love was the ingredient that was needed to make the plants grow. Some of the healers involved said that they could not cause any significant changes until they felt a caring and compassionate connection first.

An experiment by Glen Rein of Quantum Biology Research Labs in New York and Rollin McCraty of the Institute of Heartmath showed that love even allowed people to mentally influence the behaviour of DNA.

Research into gene expression has shown that genes switch on and off depending on how you are thinking or feeling, but there is no direct intention in those experiments like, "*I am visualising switching on such and such a gene now.*" (Although this should be possible, and could easily be measured!) It is always indirect in that it occurs without you willing it to happen. However the Rein and McCraty experiments showed that the feeling of love could make DNA directly respond to intention.

In their experiment, a group of people were given a jar containing DNA and were asked to try to mentally unwind the two strands while the scientists followed the behaviour of the DNA using spectroscopic techniques. Half of them had been instructed in standard Heartmath techniques for generating a genuine feeling of love and appreciation, and half of them had not been.

When the two groups were asked to try to mentally unwind the DNA strands, only the people who felt love and appreciation were able to do it. The other group had no effect. The feeling of love was vital in being able to mentally influence DNA.

This shows that, at a very deep level, healing with intention is much more likely to occur when you have a genuine wish to help.

If you show kindness, care, and compassion to everyone around you, family members, friends, colleagues, and people you come into contact with, you will have a beneficial effect on them, and on yourself. What you give out always comes back in one form or another. The love you give out will affect your own body, and your life.

Love is what is inside you, even if you don't always see it. Let it out! Kindness can be in a simple smile, or a few choice words, or saying 'yes' when someone asks you to help. It can be listening to someone who needs to talk or it can be appreciating the differences in people. Some people have a different way of doing things, which may be different from your own.

Love can be active. You don't always need to wait until you feel it. It is already inside you. Share it out a bit and you will notice that others will do the same. Your words and actions will unconsciously give people permission to rise to new heights. That can be your gift to them.

11

Mass Reality

In the same way that we participate in the creation of our bodies and influence the reality of our lives, we influence the whole world and all of the events that happen in it. Our Higher Selves manufacture the atoms and molecules but our collective daily thinking and feeling influences the process.

Have you ever seen a cartoon on TV where a depressed person is followed around by a black cloud over their head? If you feel consistently depressed then there will be a depressed mental and emotional atmosphere surrounding you, just like a black cloud. And as you are probably aware, people sense it from you just as if they could see the cloud with their eyes. In the same way you pick up on other people's moods too.

Similarly, a happy and joyful person will be surrounded by a joyful atmosphere and this will also be quite apparent to people who come into contact with him or her. Indeed, our emotional atmospheres are infectious and interact as we mix with each other.

They mix in much the same way that weather fronts mix and merge. And with a population of over six billion people there is a lot of mixing and merging going on. So a collective mental and emotional climate surrounds the world, representing the sum total of six billion or so mental and emotional climates.

Have you ever seen a satellite picture of the earth from space? You will have seen swirls of mixing clouds, some storm fronts, and some large areas of clear sky, displaying different climates all over the world. A similar picture can be drawn for the collective mental and emotional climate.

In some areas the climate might be joyful and in others it might be unhappy. In some places it might be generally positive, and there might be lots of happy people living there, and in some others the atmosphere might lean towards unhappiness.

These areas might be entire continents or they may be small and contain small groups of people, like in a household, an office, or a building, or they may even be towns or cities. And, of course, within each of these areas there will be a spread of different mental and emotional climates corresponding to the differences in people.

For instance, say the mental and emotional climate for a group or area was at level 7 out of 10, this would not mean that everyone living there was at level 7. There would be people at level 3 and 9 living there too. Taken collectively, the climate would average out at 7.

We tend to gravitate towards people and places that resonate with us; to those people and places with a similar climate to ours. You might have noticed in your own life that there are places that you have visited where you feel better or worse than usual. While you are there you might feel more positive or more peaceful, for instance, or even more anxious or agitated.

Wherever you go you are affected by the mental and emotional climate of the area. Have you ever noticed this? Felt the 'vibe' of a town or city? And just like the weather, some climates might suit you because they resonate with you and others may not, just as a warm climate may suit one person and a cold climate may suit another.

So in the same way that our unconscious minds are linked to form a collective unconscious mind, our conscious mental and emotional states form a collective mental and emotional climate state. And just as personal thoughts and emotions influence biological events in our bodies and daily events in our lives, collective thinking of a small or mass group influences local or mass events.

Group consciousness and Group Health

Group consciousness is the collective consciousness of any group; like a family, village, town, city, nation, continent, or species, and plays a role in why some places can experience positive or negative states of health. Just as a disease in the body can be a consequence of mental stress, an illness (like a cold for example) in a family group can be sustained through collective patterns of thinking and feeling within the group.

Of course this can also be easily explained by considering the food we eat, our lifestyles, and in the case of disease, of the physical spreading of viruses through contact or through the air. This is true also. There are many causes of illness, but remember that consciousness precedes biology. It condenses to form it. It is not the other way around.

Through the interconnectedness of all things, thoughts could even inspire the consciousness of disease-carrying insects to cause a harmful pathogen to be transported through the air in a particular direction.

A friend recounted a funny story to me. He was aboard an airplane and his attention was drawn to a woman at the back of the plane shouting, "*I'm going to be sick*," as she hurried towards the toilets at the front. He was having 'one of those days' where he shook his head and thought to himself, "*I'll bet she stops right at me and throws up.*" You know what? She passed dozens of people, stopped right at him, turned to face him and threw up over him.

You may have noticed that sometimes in life, according to our thoughts, feelings, beliefs, and our issues, we attract situations to ourselves like magnets. They send a pulse through the web, causing people to show up who bring us exactly what is appropriate to our current state of mind. A disease-carrying insect or an airborne pathogen will 'hear' you just as well as a person does.

Thoughts create and sustain good and poor health, individually and collectively. Mind-body effects happen collectively just as easily as they happen in individuals.

So it is just as important to deal with collective attitudes and beliefs in a group, therefore, as it is to take medication, just as you would take this approach with individuals.

But of course, this does not mean that all diseases and events are a direct product of conscious thoughts and feelings. It is very clear that a vast number of people infected with, say HIV and AIDS for instance, did not attract the disease through their thinking.

In terms of mass disease there must be a deeper, spiritual, significance as to why each person is born into such conditions, known only to the Higher Self, of which thorough investigation of their beliefs might reveal. Some hope may lie in the fact that a change of mind can cure individual disease; therefore a change of mind in a nation, through education perhaps, could save many lives.

Group consciousness affects individual consciousness and it can be very difficult to transcend the group mind and hold onto your own attitudes and beliefs. Individuals usually begin to adopt a similar mindset to the rest of the group. A mass consciousness of disease in a country will influence most of the people living in the proximity, just as living in a room with people who have flu will influence your chances of catching it.

In the same way, though, many people educated to a new mindset will influence others in the group. A mindset of health will eventually eradicate a disease, partly through its direct biological effects and also due to how it unconsciously inspires people in different parts of the world to find cures or provide aid. The bottom line is that, eventually, the strongest mindset wins! Health or disease!

Changing the World

In general, certain types of events are more likely to occur in areas where the mental and emotional climate resonates with them. Certain areas where conflict has been regular throughout history are more likely to experience fighting, then, than another area where this has not been the case.

People in such areas have known conflict so the thought of conflict is strong in the group consciousness of the city or nation. The mental and emotional climate in the area will inspire individuals with one way to resolve their differences, which may be completely alien to people in another area who are bathed in the sunshine of a different mental and emotional climate.

A change in the nature of events requires a change in the group mind in that area. History has taught us that this will most likely start with one person, or occur from within a small group of individuals, or even by the introduction of new people to the group.

But to reiterate, some events, natural disasters and epidemics among them, can have a much deeper spiritual significance where there is no apparent link between the mental and emotional climate of the area and the event. However, all must have a spiritual source, known to the Higher Self of everyone affected, which we may or may not ever consciously understand.

It is possible that a natural disaster on a very large scale, for instance, might happen so that we can grow from it, causing us to search inside of ourselves for our compassion. In the grander scheme of things then, such events were created to move the world closer to enlightenment. The Higher Selves of the individuals who lost their lives would have chosen to be part of the event, and at some level each person would have been aware in their own way. There can be no accidents in our interconnected conscious universe.

At the root, our collective Higher Selves materialise all things and events and our collective mental and emotional state influences the process. It globally influences the interface between energy vibrations and particles, shaping them and organising them into a format that accurately reflects, as events, the average state of consciousness of humanity. We get what we concentrate upon in our own lives but we also get what we concentrate upon in the world.

A world of peace and joy reflects an overall average inner climate of peace and joy, and a world where conflict is rife represents a significant degree of personal unrest and unhappiness.

Of course, this does not mean that everyone has the same influence on every event. A contented person might play only the tiniest role in the creation and sustenance of war. An average climate, say it was at level 5 out of 10 for example, is merely the average. Many people will be 2's and 3's and others will be 8's and 9's. Some people have a larger effect on certain events than others.

People who are 8's and 9's, for instance, might have more of a sustaining effect on positive events while people who were 2's and 3's might have more influence upon conflicting situations.

If you wish to change anything, therefore, then start with yourself. Examine the contents of your own mind, *honestly*, and notice what you are feeding into the collective mental and emotional climate. If there's a conflict you know of in your family group, your work environment, or in a nation, notice if you judge the people involved. Do you mentally or verbally condemn their actions? If so then you merely feed the conflict. Think about it! Perhaps not as much as those directly participating but you still play a role.

Therefore, make any changes to your own attitudes and behaviours that you believe are required, until what you project outwards is consistent with what you wish to see in the world. You will very quickly notice that the type of events in your life will change and gradually the nature of world events will also change, but it all begins with you.

You could even help others to change their mental and emotional climates too, and then you will have a greater effect on the world. This is why the peace prayers described earlier, and others like them, influence world events. As more and more people join together with their intentions, the effects become more massive. The group intentions project outwards, sending large waves along the 'web' that have a large influence upon the global mental and emotional climate, which then shapes the happenings in the world.

If many of us try to see the best in each other, forgiving where it is necessary, acting peacefully, joyfully, and kindly towards each other, then we will send large waves throughout the world. Forgiveness, peace, joy, and kindness will colour the mental and emotional atmosphere of the world, and you will find that more forgiveness, peace, joy, and kindness will be introduced to the world, even in areas remote from yourself.

If enough of us desire to help those in need, and even act on our desires with gestures as simple as flashing a genuine smile, saying something nice, making a donation, helping an elderly person with their shopping, allowing a car in front of us in a traffic jam, or even inviting someone to go in front of us in the supermarket queue, then we will find that more assistance will reach people on a global scale who might even be thousands of miles away. Our intentions will vibrate the 'web', inspiring those people who are in the right place and have the resources to offer the most help where it is needed.

It is what we project outwards that inspires others to act. It's all down to us. Each of us are far more grand, powerful, and beautiful than we have ever conceived. And yes, that means you!

How magnificent you are! You hold the power within you to change the world.

It only takes one more drop

A very small number of people can shift the mental and emotional climate in the world. Ever heard of The Butterfly Effect? A butterfly flapping its wings on one side of the world can cause a tornado at the other side. And this has been proven mathematically.

Have you heard of the 'Hundredth Monkey' experiment? It originated in 1952 when a group of scientists were studying the behaviour of monkeys on the island of Koshima, off the coast of Japan. They would feed the monkeys by dropping sweet potatoes on the sand, however the sand made the potatoes difficult to eat and eroded the teeth of the monkeys. Soon, one of the monkeys learned to wash the potatoes in the ocean and then taught some of the others to do the same. As you would expect, the practise of washing the potatoes gradually spread throughout the group. But at one point, all of a sudden, every monkey in the group started washing its food.

And at the same time, another unrelated group of scientists were studying monkeys on the mainland when they also noticed an odd change in behaviour. All of a sudden, every one of the monkeys they were studying began to wash their food. The two groups were not in contact so there was no physical way for the second band of monkeys to learn the practice.

The idea of washing food was transmitted through the group consciousness of the monkeys, inspiring monkeys on other islands to do the same things. This type of phenomenon has been well documented.

In another experiment, two sets of laboratory rats were bred through several generations by biologist W.E. Agar, in Melbourne, Australia, and were kept apart so that there was never any contact between them. One set were trained to find their way through a maze and the other set were not.

Of the set that practised the maze, one generation took twenty-five attempts, on average, to get through before the route was memorised by them. It was noted that each successive generation of rats learned slightly faster than the preceding ones, and this was attributed, at the time, to learned behaviour being genetically inherited through the DNA in each successive generation.

By the fiftieth generation the rats were getting through the maze much faster. At this point the group of rats that had not been trained, also now in their fiftieth generation, were tested on the maze. One would expect them to take about twenty-five attempts, as they did in their first generation, since none of the successive generations had experienced the maze so there could be no genetically transmitted skill. However, when this group were tested it was discovered that they made it through as fast as the rats that had inherited the ability. Yet the two groups had never met. There was no genetic opportunity for them to inherit the knowledge.

Once again, the knowledge was transmitted through the group consciousness of the rats, so that when the untrained group of rats were tested on the maze, the knowledge was 'in the air' as part of the mental and emotional climate in the area. They just downloaded it.

You may have noticed that when computers were first invented people found it difficult to understand them. Nowadays they are far more complex yet people master them very quickly, particularly children.

The knowledge has been passed along through the collective consciousness so that each successive generation of us is more confident and has an innate basic awareness of computers that is awakened when we begin to use them. Each user of a computer adds to the knowledge that's in the collective consciousness.

You might think of it as each user adding a drop of watercolour to a canvas. In time the colour becomes very deep and is highly visible, even at a distance. In the same way, the understanding of computers forms a print in the collective consciousness that becomes more 'visible' with each successive generation. Each new generation is more aware of the print because it now forms a significant part of the canvas.

Of course there are no isolated groups under study, like Agar's rats, so the learned behaviour is also genetically transmitted. Both occur, but not just the genetic inheritance as has been previously assumed.

Information travels fast through the collective unconscious and in the collective mental and emotional climate. It is instantly available everywhere. But although it is instantly available it usually takes a little longer to be downloaded because of people's personal mental and emotional noise - their thoughts and emotions, their attitudes, and their beliefs - just like it takes anyone longer to 'get the point' about something if they have a lot on their mind.

Usually the information is gradually downloaded into more and more people until a certain amount is reached, called a 'critical' or 'tipping' point. But once the point is reached the information appears to download into everyone else simultaneously.

This is how critical points work. Levels increase gradually until a specific point is reached then change is extremely rapid. Think of it like more and more weight being added to a set of balance scales. When the weight reaches a certain amount, the tipping point, the scales tip over to the other side.

It is well known in the weather as sudden changes occur due to the reaching of a critical point of air pressure, storm density, wind speed, temperature, or other phenomenon. In the Hollywood movie, 'The Day After Tomorrow', a tipping point was reached in the degree of polar icecap melting. Once this point was reached there was no turning back. Changes happened extremely rapidly. In just over a week it sent the entire planet into an ice age. The global mental and emotional climate can shift in this way too, although, spiritually, it appears to be moving towards a 'golden age' and not an ice age.

There are certain types of biological experiments that show the same thing. Bacteria A is slowly transforming into B then all of a sudden, when the transformation reaches a certain point, it flicks over to completion. In some cases, a critical amount can be a very small number and in other cases it can be large. Many vital protein and enzyme transformations in the body happen in this way.

Analytical chemists also see it. They use 'indicators' which detect when an acid-alkali titration is complete. It is a standard experiment that is carried out from high schools to university research labs to analytical laboratories in the healthcare industry.

Lots of drops of A can be added to B and the mixture remains colourless then suddenly, with the addition of only one or two more drops of A (close to the tipping point) the entire mixture turns pink in an instant. It is not a gradual change in colour; it is an instant change.

And so it is with the mixture of our mental and emotional climates. If we consistently add drops of peace and love, kindness and sharing, tolerance and understanding, through our attitudes and behaviours towards each other, then once we collectively reach a critical mass of people behaving in this way, things in the world will noticeably change very quickly.

There will be more peace, love, kindness, sharing, tolerance, and understanding in the world because vast amounts of people will be inspired with these qualities simultaneously. Every drop is important. And you wondered how important you were!

Just prior to the tipping point it only takes one more drop for the colour to change. Without that drop it never changes. You don't need to do big things to change the world; you only need to change yourself.

The changes in the world will be profound, because world events mirror our collective climate. This is not to say that this will happen, only that it can happen. We need to do the work.

Nothing happens by itself, just as no molecule in the body randomly creates itself. A determined positive attitude creates good health and positive life experiences, and when many of us focus our thoughts in this way it inspires positive world events.

And the same, of course, happens when we dwell on what is not desirable or mentally and verbally condemn the actions of another on a consistent basis.

Focusing on your distaste for war and the decisions surrounding it, for example, will not bring lasting peace. Although you admirably intend peace, you also feed the conflict. Three steps forward, two steps back. By now you should understand that a love of peace, all that it represents, and a demonstration of peace in your own life, is a more efficient formula for lasting peace. Therefore, a 'for-peace' rally carries far more positive power than an anti-war one.

Tolerance and willingness to try to understand the actions of another makes more of a lasting contribution towards peace than a desire for peace fuelled with a hatred of war and all that it represents. St. Francis of Assisi once said, "*Seek first to understand, then to be understood.*" This is the key to peace in your personal life and in the world. Seek first to understand people before making a judgement, where you probably don't know all of the facts.

Can you absolutely know something to be true? Like why someone did what he or she did. Or are you making an assumption based upon what you've heard, or based upon your own past experience? Because the assumption you make determines the quality of your life, your relationships, and the quality of intention you transmit into the world, which then inspires others. Many of us have unknowingly perpetrated conflicts around us in this way.

Furthermore, you know what you do to your body with consistent negative thinking so what do you suppose we do to the body-of-the-world every day when millions of us focus on what is not looking good, and go through our days in mental and emotional conflict with one another?

It is impossible for you not to affect your body, your life, or the world by the way you think and act. You cannot disentangle yourself from any of it. You are intimately connected to every atom. How you affect things then, from this moment onwards, depends on the choices you make today.

If you find yourself consistently reacting angrily to something or someone, try to stop for a minute and ask yourself what contribution such behaviour makes to the world. Then find a way of healing your thoughts, attitudes, and beliefs.

The next time you find yourself speaking negatively about someone behind their back, stop and ask yourself what you will be doing to them, and what contribution your words are making to the world.

You are important and your thoughts, feelings, and words are extremely powerful. Far more so than you ever imagined!

Who you choose to be from this moment onwards will affect the world. So who do you choose to be?

12

DNA - II

We have learned from earlier chapters that our Higher Selves create the subatomic particles that form our atoms, which go on to form our proteins, enzymes, and DNA, as well as the cells and the entire physical structure of our bodies.

DNA is the genetic blueprint that determines what we look like, but the Higher Self provides the mental blueprint that precedes it, determining the actual physical structure of our DNA.

Many people believe that the mind is a product of chemical interactions in the brain. Indeed, scientific studies have shown that alterations to the brain cause perception and behavioural changes. But this is only half of the story. Mind *is* influenced by chemical interactions in the brain but it originates *beyond* biology. The spirit flows *through* the body. Its flow is affected by the state of the body, giving us the impression that it is a product of biology.

Our genetic blueprint is merely a filter that allows a certain intensity of spirit to influence the body and mind. The Higher self chooses the genetic filter so that a life may be experienced within a certain context.

Life is like a painting. The Higher Self chooses the canvas and the colours but we create the picture.

The mental blueprint of the Higher Self condenses into the chosen 'colours' of DNA. Its thought waves (vibrations) condense into particles that form patterns that organise into matter that become the genes of your DNA. Prior to vibrations there is stillness, just like still water when there is no wind. In this state, nothing exists. Only perfect stillness.

But then an idea is had and just as a pebble dropped into the water produces waves, the idea forms vibrations in the 'field', which then condense to form the particles that eventually produce the image of the idea. These vibrations are the mental blueprint that determines what you will look like, and the condensed particles organise themselves accordingly so that appropriate genes are present in your DNA when you are no more than a single cell in the womb, predisposed to switch on and off so that you can grow into the image held by your Higher Self.

Perhaps it was God's idea to form the universe. This idea made quite a lot of vibrations that have condensed into everything you see around you! This might then be the symbolic root of the passage from The New Testament that says:

"In the beginning was the Word and the Word was with God, and the Word was God." **John 1:1.** A word is an idea vocalised, and when you vocalise any sound you create vibrations. That is what a sound is, pure vibrations. A word is the vibrating sound of the vowels and consonants. Vibrations of sound are larger and more intense than the vibrations of mental images. That is probably the only significant difference. The word 'God' (symbolising God creating) made vibrations in the stillness that resulted in the creation of the universe.

This is why some mystics chant the name God, or the sound 'Om' or 'Ah', and why the name of God has the 'O' or 'Ah' sound in many different cultures in the world. It is said that the ancient mystics and sages vocalised the sounds of creation they heard during deep meditation, revealing the name of the creator in the language of that culture. The sound of God is, therefore, said to be the sound of creation. This is also the root of the mantra-based meditation practises that use the 'Om' sound. These sounds help the practitioner to have a conscious experience of God.

So the genes that we are born with are principally the products of choice by our Higher Selves. They are also, however, inherited from our parents. And there is no contradiction here.

Similarities probably exist in families because the Higher Selves have chosen to be similar. Our human families are perhaps families of Higher Selves who think alike, and so form similar vibrations with their ideas. What we see as similar genes, in accordance with the laws of genetics and inheritance, is no more than the end product of a creative series of events that originated with similar ideas.

I believe that each Higher Self chooses particular genes within the framework of what is possible within such laws.

Therefore we are born with certain genes that are predisposed (intended) to switch on at certain times throughout our lives to give us certain characteristics and to lead us into certain types of experiences desired by our Higher Selves. You could say that instructions for our unique mental, physical, and spiritual growth are 'imprinted' into our DNA, predisposing certain genes to switch on and off at certain times and so predisposing us towards certain characteristics and certain types of experiences. These imprints are deep psychological ones representing the mental blueprints of the Higher Self.

Anyone can become aware of some of these mental blueprints, particularly the ones relating to our purpose in life. Do you ever feel that you have a purpose that you are just not living? Or maybe you are living it. These feelings are the blueprints of the Higher Self. I believe living our purpose allows maximum flow of spirit through the body, and that is why people who are living their purpose tend to feel joyful most of the time.

Your purpose doesn't need to be something big. As many people begin to embrace spiritual concepts they quite often feel that their purpose is to change the world single handed. This is usually, however, really a feeling of the awesome power of consciousness available to them. From my own experience they are often sensing an increased flow of spirit through their body, and undoubtedly a new program of genes switching on and off accompanies this. Your purpose may be subtler than this or maybe your purpose is to have an obviously huge impact on the world.

Many people have a purpose to bring children into the world, others to act, to write books, to teach, to sing, to dance, to cook, to clean, to heal, to be peaceful, to cause chaos, to lead, or to follow.

Parents will probably notice that their children have certain abilities from an early age. They might be highly intelligent, or great at sports, or really creative, or copy performers on the TV with great accuracy, or they might act like little doctors or nurses or even teachers. Some may have a fascination for cars, or why things work the way they do. This is no accident. It is their purpose condensed into their DNA beginning to assert itself.

And we may have more than one purpose. As we fulfil one, the next takes precedence.

Why not ask your Higher Self what your purpose is! It may come to you in a flash of inspiration a day or two later or events may just transpire that nudge you into what you are meant to do.

Conscious Evolution

Vibrations are consistent throughout every part of our existence. The earth rotates about the sun forming the cycle (vibration) of one year, the moon rotates about the earth forming the cycle of one month, and the earth rotates on its axis forming the cycle of one day. Our bodies also work on cycles.

In the science of genetics it is well known that many genes switch on an off in waves, according to clock rhythms and cycles; for example genes that are involved in sleep.

Cycles cause us to physically develop the way we do. The brain, for instance, undergoes cyclic spurts of growth at birth, and approximately at ages 1, 4, 7, 11, 15, and 21; each spurt involving waves of gene expression. The growth of the central nervous system has also been shown to take place through periodic waves of gene expression. Puberty and menopause are the results of longer-term cycles.

Vibrations must have an ultimate cause. I believe that our internal body cycles are a consequence of the Higher Self's thought vibrations. Such vibrations will ultimately be the source of why certain genes are predisposed to switch on and off at specific times.

In a similar way, the idea for the human race created a vibration in the stillness of the 'field'. You could call it the 'vibration of the human race'. The existence of such a vibration explains why there is a similarity in shape among all of us, in that most of us have two arms, two legs, two eyes, a mouth, etc. The vibration ensures consistency in human DNA.

What we call genetic mutations, and the associated deformities, are not mistakes. In fact they are the results of decisions by Higher Selves.

A person who is physically, or even mentally different, whether from a genetic difference or otherwise, should therefore never be considered less than anyone else. I believe that it takes a brave and enlightened Soul (Higher Self) to choose genetic characteristics that cause it to be labelled different in unenlightened times.

What is normal is not what is right. It is just what most Higher Selves have chosen. No more, no less.

The human race has evolved over millions of years so the 'vibration of the human race' has been constantly changing (in small ways). In some ways it is speeding up now as tolerance, kindness, and compassion flood throughout the world in greater amounts than ever before. As the collective mental and emotional climate changes it sends intentions (which are vibrations) to the point where vibrations condense into particles. These collective thoughts and feelings resonate with, and entrain, the vibration in the same way that a tuning fork will cause a guitar string to vibrate to its tone. So this gives us a degree of influence upon our own evolution.

The evolution of humanity, then, is the result of a changing vibration, moving from a low frequency towards a higher frequency, or vice versa depending upon the collective choices we make, just as sound changes when we pluck a different note on a guitar string.

As we collectively make higher choices, ones that are based upon greater spiritual principles like tolerance, kindness, and compassion, we produce higher vibrations that in turn entrain the collective vibration to a higher frequency. Each time, the string of humanity plays a higher note.

And it goes the other way too. As the collective vibration increases in frequency it inspires us, influencing the choices we make to be consistent with its vibrations. We are evolving in the way we look at the world and in our sense of connection to one another in the human family. Look at the world. It is really obvious.

And each time the vibration shifts, it is not only our thoughts and emotions that are affected. Biology must shift too.

Of course I am not talking of obvious physical changes, although these might await us in the very distant future. I am referring to minor alterations in which genes are on and off, leading to relatively minor biological changes. These will simply mirror the way in which humanity collectively views each other and their place in the world.

It must be happening in people alive at present. Some may find their bodies no longer tolerating old eating habits, for instance, developing unexplained allergies to foods that are unhealthy. Others may find themselves experiencing greater psychological stress as the new vibration brings to the surface old mental and emotional issues that need resolving, and remind us of people we need to forgive. Still others may experience stress-related illnesses as they resist the inner urge to make alterations to their way of life, perhaps to take a step towards embracing their life's purpose.

Others still may simply be feeling emotionally better and better every day and noticing that their bodies are becoming fitter and healthier.

All *apparently* negative psychological and physical experiences are simply psychological and biological adjustments to the higher vibration and may then be viewed as 'healing in progress'.

What is really interesting is that the higher vibration will also influence our future children's DNA because it will condense from the 'vibration of the human race'. If we choose more tolerance, kindness, compassion, and peace for instance (what we seem to be doing) – a collective increase in love – our children will be born with a greater predisposition towards love, peace, and spiritual growth. In this way, our choices today affect the future state of the world.

Each of us has a great responsibility, then, not only to ourselves, but also to our children so that they have a chance to live in a world free of poverty, war, and injustices, but instead a world filled with sharing, cooperation, tolerance, compassion, achievement, education, kindness, and peace.

I have heard some stories, and I believe some of them because it makes sense in the context of what I have written here, that a number of children are being born with a higher level of immunity to some of our most serious diseases. This may be explained in purely genetic terms, but consciousness precedes biology.

If the vibration level of humanity had evolved, say, twenty points in the last twenty years then children being born now will have slightly different DNA (perhaps not so much in the genes they have but in the patterns of which genes are on and off) from children born twenty years ago. I am quite sure that scientists could find ways to verify this.

As we are collectively evolving a wiser spiritual understanding regarding the interconnectedness of all things, we are slowly transcending old mental and emotional habits. It follows, therefore, that we are probably also evolving physical resistance to some of the diseases that collectively mirrored these old habits.

Just as many people contract disease, many more will have developed immunity that they, and others, may never realise they have. If researchers are looking for chemical or biological cures for some of these diseases it could be that they need look no further than healthy people.

Group Illnesses

Epidemics can spread quickly around the world. But there can also be a strong placebo effect that helps in their spread. Many of us buy into the thought of the epidemic, and secretly believe that we will catch whatever disease is going. And this is aided by advertisements that proclaim, *"one in three people will catch such and such in their lifetime."*

If a doctor approached a group of patients and said that 'this' tablet will cure one in three of them, even though it was secretly a placebo, then there's a good chance that approximately one in three will be cured.

Of course, advertisements of this nature are not intended to cause disease. It is the exact opposite. People are inherently trying to make the world a better place. The manufacturers of drugs are trying to defeat diseases, and so are the research and development scientists whose passion and life's purpose is to help sick people. Advertisements of this nature are not created with conscious awareness of the suggestions that they give to people. They simply use current statistics, but statistics can be misleading if their details are not fully understood.

They can create a local or global placebo effect that inspires people to believe that they will contract such and such a disease. Their body's biochemistry naturally mirrors this so that the statistics have a chance of becoming self-fulfilling.

Such a placebo effect might work by switching on viruses and bacteria already present in the body, giving us 'ghost' symptoms, or even causing us to unconsciously 'call out' to airborne pathogens.

Most of us have traces of most viruses and bacteria, and even the deadliest ones, in our bodies. Yet they lie dormant, doing no harm, in fact they probably play a cameo role in keeping health and balance in the body. Believing a disease suggestion might switch them on, making a usually harmless virus into a deadly virus. Other people without traces of the virus may simply develop symptoms, according to those beliefs, that may turn out to be as harmful as the actual virus. And of course, there is also an obvious spread through touch or through the air.

So in some cases, it might not be so much the virus that is the disease as it is the thoughts, emotions, and beliefs that create them, guide them, and activate them that is the disease.

On a global scale the spread of an epidemic could be amplified by mental and emotional patterns throughout an entire nation or culture. It could happen in the same way that families and groups of people sharing similar attitudes and beliefs often develop the same illnesses.

Although, obviously there are many different direct causes for diseases that are unrelated to conscious thoughts and feelings.

For example, diet, toxins, poisons, genetic inheritance, transmitted viruses and bacteria, and even electromagnetic fields, to name just a few. There is not always a large role of consciousness just as there is not always a large placebo effect in the treatment of some illnesses. But, however large or small, it cannot be ignored.

Another aspect of the role of consciousness is that collective thoughts can affect people all over the world who are unaware of what is going on.

Just as intentions or emotions can bring about an effect in our own body, or in someone else's that we are consciously or unconsciously thinking about, our collective mental and emotional patterns might unconsciously project an illness, or symptoms of an illness, onto people spread out all over the world.

For instance, atmospheric pollution and destruction of oxygen-producing rainforests can damage the 'lungs' of the planet. On an unconscious level we are all aware of this because the knowledge vibrates the 'web'.

So it would make sense if there were an increase in the number of respiratory diseases (e.g. asthma or TB) showing up all over the world just as consistent thoughts of damaged lungs in an individual might bring about such a condition, or symptoms of the condition, in that person.

Most of those people with respiratory difficulties would not have attracted the illness through any conscious way of thinking of their own (although their Higher Self is well aware of what is going on and will have reasons of its own that may or may not be conscious in the individuals). And in some individuals with respiratory conditions theirs will be entirely unrelated. As I have indicated already, there are many competing factors that cause illnesses.

In the same way, there might be a link between reduction of biodiversity by man-made extinction of species, which can damage the 'immune system' of the planet, and an increase in numbers of people developing suppressed immune systems, allergies, and related diseases. The conscious and unconscious awareness of these happenings can project outwards, showing up in people anywhere in the world.

Similarly, those affected did not attract the disease through any fault of their own but their Higher Self undoubtedly has a reason for them to have developed it.

But, *in general*, the way we personally think and feel can create or cure a disease and can affect how fast or slow a disease works its way through our bodies and, *in general*, our collective mental and emotional climates can do the same on a larger scale.

Just as we can activate viruses we should also be able to deactivate them, then, just as our thoughts and feeling can switch our own genes on and off. Perhaps we can collectively generate a positive placebo effect around the fact that "We are healthy!"

Maybe the media could help. With faith in this we would develop a degree of mental, and therefore physical, immunity.

As a consequence of our evolution in consciousness, it is likely that some people are already psychologically, and therefore physically, immune to some diseases, and even if they contract them through the air their imprints will immediately neutralise them. Such individuals likely exist, it is just that we are not generally aware of them and neither are they aware of their own immunities.

There is a habitual tendency in many of us, most of the time, to only notice something when it goes wrong, and give little attention to things that are going right. We often focus more on disease than health, and so inspiring within ourselves what we most concentrate upon. We would be better to do the opposite and focus some more of our attention on health and the reasons why people are healthy.

We get what we concentrate upon, individually and collectively. If we change our minds about the world, looking to the beauty and qualities of human spirit around us, the spirit of compassion and kindness inherent in everyone, then we will get more of that.

Our health, and our world, is more in our hands than we have ever imagined. So let us appreciate each other and be kind to each other, and collectively we can make our world into the type of world whose existence is encoded in our genes.

13

Personal Responsibility

Each of us plays an important role in the world regardless of our status, how much money we have, where we live, what we do for a living, whether we are married or single, whether we have children, or whether we are children.

Every one of your thoughts, emotions, ideas, and dreams contribute to painting the landscape of humanity. Together we make the world the way it is. There is no one more important or less important than you, only people with different roles. There is no one more a part of the world or less a part of the world than you.

There is no one who doesn't contribute to the world, regardless of where he or she lives or what physical role they appear to be playing, because it is not possible to be separate from the world. Your presence on the planet adds intelligence to the collective consciousness so it affects the world. Every drop of water in the ocean is important to the ocean because it is part of the ocean. Without it, it wouldn't be the same ocean.

It is not unusual to look at someone and think, "*How magnificent you are.*" But there is someone, somewhere, looking in your direction thinking the same thing about you.

If we want the world to be different then it is up to us to take personal responsibility for it. Each intention, positive or negative, contributes to the whole. Just as creating a website changes the information content of the internet, your intentions change the information content of the 'web' and influence events, large and small, in the world.

It is not harmful to have negative thoughts or painful emotions, even though we are well aware of their effects.

It is often the case that people experience pain in order to jump up into a positive state. Therefore the pain was important to them. And we know it does little good to suppress mental and emotional pain. Hiding it does not negate its affects.

Every thought and emotion, value and belief, idea and dream, is valid. Even seemingly negative ones because they can sometimes provide positive inspiration for others. Seeing someone acting negatively might cause another to think, "*I sometimes do that, but now I see what it looks like and the effects it has on other people so I resolve, now, to change.*"

It is important, also, not to judge the person acting in this way. To do so is to shows a lack of compassion for another's pain, and is also to condemn yourself! Everyone has a place in the world and together we make it exactly the way it is.

Consistency is the key to lasting change. What we consistently project outwards has a more lasting effect. If you want to see a world you dream of, firstly examine the contents of your own mind and take note of what you are projecting outwards on a consistent basis. Secondly, work on resolving your own personal suffering. And finally, bring your thoughts, attitudes, and actions into alignment with the type of thing you wish to see in the world.

Through taking such personal responsibility for our consistent thoughts, attitudes, and behaviours we can collectively create a beautiful world for our children and our children's children. If we can learn to consistently see the world through wiser eyes, seeing its beauty and the inner beauty of all people, then we will get more of it. This can be the legacy that we leave for them.

Each of us, individually, is much more important and powerful than we believe ourselves to be. It is because most of us don't realise our power that we keep on thinking and behaving in the same way.

Many of us condemn events that are undesirable, berating people for not doing anything to change stuff, all the while never realising that we, through our attitude, have a constant hand in their creation. Through our attitudes, what we project outwards provides the food that nourishes people doing the very things we disapprove of.

We would do better to simply notice what is undesirable and then say, "*I love...*", whatever the opposite might be. For example, seeing war as undesirable, you might want to say, "*I love peace,*" instead of "*I hate war*", then be peaceful (and joyful) in your interactions with people. "*I hate war,*" reveals a different path from "*I love peace,*" and so there are different consequences in your personal lives and in the world. Also, try to focus on examples of peace in your personal life and in the world because what you focus on you get more of.

It would also be good to search for the place within you that houses forgiveness, and practise forgiving people for any wrongs you believe they have done to you or to the world.

If you have difficulty in doing any of these things then seek a suitable resource, book, counsellor, therapist, or teacher, who can guide you to changing inner beliefs because it is our inner beliefs that cause us to think in particular ways. One such book I would recommend is *"Loving What Is"* by Byron Katie.

Being mindful like this is taking personal responsibility for your own life and for the part you play in the world.

You are an unseen inspiration to people all over the world, even if you don't realise it. Who you choose to be, today, will impact on people that you come into contact with and, through our interconnectedness, people who you do not. It is who you choose to be now that matters. So who do you choose to be?

14

Three Simple Rules

There are three simple rules that you can live by which can make you happy, which can inspire happiness in those around you, and that can change the world. These are: love for self, love for others, and love for nature.

Rule 1
Love for Self

Have you ever said to someone, "*I love you just the way you are*"? And I'll bet you meant it, because we have a great capacity to see the best in each other.

Love for self is saying, "*I love myself just the way I am.*" You are just as special as anyone else. In God's eyes we are equally, and infinitely, loved.

Try to stop criticising yourself. Try to stop beating yourself up for what you should or shouldn't have done. And try to stop blaming yourself for things that have happened in the past.

A child learns from its mistakes but shouldn't be condemned for making them. It was a part of the process of learning, of evolution. On a spiritual scale, we are all children and will inevitably make mistakes. It's part of the process.

I once heard the author, Dr Wayne Dyer, tell a story of how trappers used to catch monkeys in the jungle. They would set down a large heavy jar containing sweet nuts in an area that monkeys lived. The jar had a narrow neck, just wide enough for a monkey's arm so that it could reach in to take the nuts.

When the monkey comes along it reaches into the jar and grabs the nuts. But its tightening grip makes its hand too wide to get out of the jar. It tries and tries but it can't get its hand out of the jar, unless it lets go of the nuts.

But it won't let go of the nuts, even though it is stuck. And the jar is so heavy that the monkey can't drag it to a different place. The trappers return the next day and catch the monkey, trapped with its hand in the jar holding the nuts. It had been there all night, never having let go of the nuts and therefore being unable to move.

This is what we tend to do in our personal lives. We hold on to things that happened in the past, playing them over and over in our minds, blaming ourselves, or others, and refusing to let go. This makes us heavy and unable to move forward in our lives. We trap ourselves.

Your Higher Self forgives all because there was never anything to forgive. It was just the process of evolution of life, driven by the vast cogs of interconnectedness. It was all stuff that happened when you were a child growing into an adult.

My friend Bruce MacKay once said to me, while we were in the mountains of Peru, "*Where are you?*" Bemused and trying to be funny I said something along the lines of "*I am on a path in the mountains of Peru.*" To this he replied, "*No. You are here.*" He then said, "*What time is it?*" As I looked to my watch he said, "*It is now. You are here, and the time is now.*"

There is only one time. It is now. In ten minutes time it will be a new now, but it is still now. The present moment is where you are now and you are right where you are. In this moment, now, you are deeply loved. You don't need to wait until some future time to be loved, or until you have committed a hundred selfless acts. You are loved now, you have always been loved, and you will always be loved.

If I pointed to someone and said that they were created out of the 'nothingness' with a breath of the pure love, how would you regard them from that moment on? I'll bet you would see he or she as a truly divine being, holding them in extremely high esteem, imagining them to be a wonderful spiritual being who is truly blessed and has a destiny to bring more love into the world.

I am pointing at you. You are that person! You who is reading this book! Out of energy vibrations, your form was created with God's loving breath. God's love is in every cell of your body, regardless of whether you believe it or not.

I once heard a story about a woman who didn't feel loved or important. A friend came to her house one day and learned of how she felt. His attention was drawn to the family pictures on her mantelpiece so he asked who was in the pictures.

She smiled as she explained that it was her children and her grandchildren, and how deeply proud she was of them, taking time to proudly list their achievements. He then looked at her and said, *"God has a picture of you on his mantelpiece."*

There's a little trick that can help you to develop love for yourself. It is called 'being kind to yourself', and it's fun.

Treat yourself to what you really want. Spoil yourself. Take a long bath with some candles and oils burning around you. Have a massage or have a healing treatment. Get your hair done or get a new image. If you don't have the resources or ability to do these things then try to find something, which is possible for you, that would be really special. Maybe there's something you love to do but haven't done for a while.

As you do any of these things, do so with the thought, *"I am a great and wonderful divine being, I am deeply loved, I love myself, and I deserve this."*

Rule 2

Love for Others

We have an amazing capacity to see the best in each other. As often as you can, then, try to see the best in the person right in front of you.

See the best in family members, friends, work colleagues, people you come into contact with throughout the day, people at meetings, clients, children, even people you regard as enemies, and people who have hurt you in the past.

All of these people, like you, were born out of the nothingness with God's loving breath. We are all brothers and sisters in the human family, but our collective mental and emotional climate has made it difficult for us to always remember this. So it is quite normal for our actions to reflect something different. But is doesn't have to be that way.

When you make an effort to see the best in someone you help to bring it out in them. I used to be an athletics coach and I could only bring out the best in the athletes when I made an effort to recognise their uniqueness. When I saw it I could point it out to them, causing them to see it too. When they saw it, it became more obvious and they were able to develop it. It works the same way with qualities of character.

If someone told you that you were a generous person then after some thought, and maybe some mental replaying of past times, you would probably think to yourself, *"Hey, I am a generous person"*, and with that thought foremost in your mind you would probably go through your day being even more generous than normal, touching many lives along the way. Pointing out great qualities in people can change the world because you encourage people to be more like who they really are.

You could notice that someone occasionally shows kindness. Try to let that be how you define them in the future. "*Oh there goes that kind person*", instead of, "*There goes so and so. Have you heard the gossip?*" My friend Stuart Wilkie used to say, "*If you have nothing nice to say then don't say anything at all.*"

How you label a person is not who they are. It is just your label, based upon your limited connection with them. If you took the time to look inside, even get to know them, you would see something very different. He or she is deeply loved, just as you are, and is your brother or sister in the human family.

You might notice that they are a great parent, or a good communicator, or that they have a nice smile, nice hair, or even that you like their choice of clothes today. Be creative. You can always make time to see something positive in another that might help them to feel better about themselves.

It might even be difficult to see something positive in their behaviour because circumstances have influenced some people so much that this part of them is buried. But you can look for it. Help them to remember.

Sometimes behaviours can cloud the truth. But no matter how many clouds are there the human spirit never ceases to shine from behind them. My partner, Elizabeth Caproni (the actress), reminded me once that an airplane might take off on a cloudy day, but as it rises above the clouds it reaches a place where the sun always shines.

Love always shines from within. It is up to you to rise above what is facing you and see it.

The actor David Hayman, a dear friend of mine, once said to me, while describing someone who brought lots of conflict into the room with him: "*He is an angel of God.... Cleverly disguised as an asshole.*" Which part are you willing to see?

If a person has hurt you in the past, try to let it go. Try to forgive them. Try to see the 'light from within' or the 'angel of God' part of them. They have merely forgotten who they really are.

Jesus said, "*Forgive them father. For they know not what they do.*" If a person does not know who he or she really is then ultimately they 'know not what they do'. Of course they must take responsibility for their own actions, but from this mindset, and in the present moment, it means that you have an opportunity to forgive and move on. Mark Twain wrote, "*Forgiveness is the fragrance that the violet sheds on the heel that has crushed it.*" Why not choose to be a violet today?

In 2004 I read in a national newspaper that a brother and sister wrote to a judge who was about to impose sentence on the driver of a truck who had killed their parents. It was a plea to him not to imprison the driver for his accident.

It brought tears to the judge's eyes as he read the letter aloud in court, emphasising the extraordinary capacity for forgiveness that the brother and sister had shown.

If all of us followed their example the world would transform overnight. Overnight! We would surpass the 'critical forgiveness point.' So do you choose to forgive or do you choose to sue? For your actions define you and colour the mental and emotional climate of the world, inspiring others everywhere to follow your example.

Forgiveness is a beautiful thing. So is kindness. Genuine kindness, in particular, carries extraordinary power. So when you do kind things for people - when you share, or speak highly of them - it is important that you mean what you do.

For example, sharing your resources with someone in need is very powerful when done with a genuine heartfelt wish to help but less powerful if done in order to gain something else.

Of course, it is not wrong to be aware that you will gain out of a kind act because there will always be a gain for you. You cannot avoid that. You get back what you give out in one form or another. Give kindness and you will receive kindness in some way.

The point is to be kind, not in order to get something back, but from a genuine heartfelt wish to help. Then your act carries much more weight. As my mum always told me as a child, *"It's the thought that counts."* The reason for doing something colours the act.

In the bible it is written, *"I may speak with the words of men and of angels, but if I have not love I am but a resounding gong or a clanging cymbal."* **I Corinthians 13**. Examine your motivations!

Anonymous acts of kindness have a huge impact. There was a time, a few years ago, that I was extremely short of money. One day I received an envelope in the post containing twenty pounds. There was no name or address, only a small piece of paper saying *"God Bless."* Whoever sent it knew of my situation but had no need for me to know of their kindness. They only wanted to help.

That twenty pounds was like a lottery win to me, and it meant more and stretched further because of the love that came with it. The spirit of the gift was far more important to me than its monetary value.

And so it is with your genuinely kind thoughts, words, and actions. The spirit of your intentions carry the power.

Have you ever seen the movie *"Pay it Forward?"* It featured a young boy who was set a school project that asked him to come up with a plan as to how he could make a difference in the world.

His plan was to commit a very special act of kindness for three people, an act that could make a real difference in their lives. When each person wished to show their gratitude he said that he didn't wish for them to repay kindness to him, but to find three people whose lives they could each make a difference in and help those people instead. In this way they were to 'Pay it Forward.'

They, in turn, could do something kind for three others, who help three others, who help three others, and so on. Each time a person who had been helped wished to show their gratitude they were also asked to pay it forward.

It is a truly inspirational film and I encourage you to watch it, or to read the book. It shows the power a person can have to make a real difference in the world through one or two simple acts of kindness.

The power to change the world is in you. All you need to do is forgive and be kind and you might just inspire others to do the same. A wave of forgiveness or kindness can be magical!

Rule 3
Love for Nature

In Thom Hartmann's bestselling book, *"The Prophet's Way"*, he describes watching his teacher, Gottfried Müller, outside on the road at 5.30am picking up dozens of small earthworms that had come to the surface during the previous night's rainfall. He was giving them a few words of comfort and reassurance and returning them to the grass so they wouldn't be run over by cars.

Herr Müller showed that love for these tiny, helpless, creatures was as important as love for each other. He had being making these anonymous acts of compassion for years yet never telling anyone.

It is not so much the act, but the quality of intentions that we act *with* - the space within us that an act comes from - that is important. Compassion is compassion is compassion, regardless of who, or what, it is directed towards. Often the greatest acts of compassion are anonymous because the act is completely genuine, undiluted by even the smallest need for recognition.

Have you ever noticed the love that a puppy shows for everyone around it? There is a puppy inside all animals, even when it is not apparently obvious. There is the same infant-spirit in the flowers and the trees, and in the insects and the fish.

Try to see the life and the beauty in nature all around you and you will help to bring it out, to flower it so to speak. What we focus on we get more of. Focus on beauty and you will create more around you.

How you choose to consistently interact with nature, from this moment on, will impact your life and the world. Love is love is love regardless of who, or what, you show love towards. Every act projects outwards, colouring the collective unconscious and influencing the world.

The question is 'what type of world do you choose'?

In Closing

You are more beautiful than you have ever believed yourself to be. You are a part of God that can never, ever, be separate from God. This infinite source of all things is in every cell in your body and is revealed in every moment of your life.

Your Higher Self is a fragment of God, simply more aware of its heritage than you are but no more a part of God than you are. In helping you to recognise who you are it has encoded a general theme for your life into your DNA, so that you have an infinite number of unique opportunities to experience your godliness.

This theme is your life's purpose. Try to discover it. Look within yourself for what brings you most joy and that is where you will find it.

You are very important to all of us. Every thought, word, or act sends ripples throughout your body and also throughout the world, making an unseen difference in the lives of people close to you and even in people far remote from you. Of these, it is not as much your thoughts, words, and actions that are important, as it is the place within you that they come from. It's the thought that counts. The thought underneath the thought is most important.

Helping someone who is poor from a genuine space of compassion is far more powerful than doing so out of a sense of guilt, or out of a desire to be recognised for you kindness.

In the same way, intentionally crushing an insect has a destructive effect. It is the space within you that an act comes from, however insignificant it may seem to you, that is important. It's the thought that counts.

The world changes as we change. It can't do anything else because it is part of us.

Look at yourself, then, honestly. Honestly! Examine your thoughts, feelings, attitudes, beliefs, and your behaviour. Then make any changes to yourself that you believe are necessary until what you project outwards is consistent with what you wish to see in your life, and in the world.

Your degree of honesty with yourself will determine the speed of the changes, and how profound they are. Eventually you will truly take on board who you really are because there will be nothing more to reveal.

And as we learn to see God in ourselves, in everyone else, and in every*thing* else, we make an even more beautiful world. Try to live by the three simple rules that respect this: Love for Self, Love for Others, and Love for Nature.

Try to see the love – the kindness, compassion, honesty, forgiveness, and gratitude – all around you, regardless of how well it is hidden. See that the world is already beautiful and, in so doing, choose more of the beauty than the pain. You don't need to hate the pain. You only need to choose something else.

Simply choose love, choose peace, choose kindness, choose honesty, and extend your hand in forgiveness and trust. Let these new choices colour the actions of your life from this day onwards. Then you will see the beauty and magnificence that is already present around you, and you will believe that all things are indeed perfect.

Such faith can move mountains!

References

Chapter 1 – Mind and Body

For effects of positive and negative emotions on the heart and immune system, see:

1. R. McCraty, M. Atkinson, W. A. Tiller, G. Rein, and A. D. Watkins, 'The effects of emotions on short-term power spectrum analysis of heart rate variability,' *Am. Journal of Cardiology*, 1995, 76, 1089-1093.

2. G. Rein, M. Atkinson, and R. McCraty, 'The physiological and psychological effects of compassion and anger', *J. Advancement in Med.*, 1995, 8(2), 87-105.

3. Janice K. Kiecolt-Glaser, Lynanne McGuire, Theodore F. Robles, and Ronald Glaser, 'Emotions, Morbidity, and Mortality: New perspectives from psychoneuroimmunology,' *Annual Rev. Psychol.*, 2002, 53, 83-107.

For general information on mind-body medicine see Deepak Chopra MD, *Quantum Healing – Exploring The Frontiers Of Mind/Body Medicine*, (Bantam, New York, 1989) and Larry Dossey MD, *Healing Beyond the Body*, (Time Warner, London, 2001).

For Effects of laughter on health see:

1. For a general review of the physiological effects of laughter see W. F. Fry, 'The physiological effects of humour, mirth, and laughter,' *Journal of the American Medical Association*, 1992, 267(13), 1857-1858.

2. Laughter improves the immune system. Increases found in natural killer cell activity and levels of some immunoglobulins, with immunoglobulin increases lasting up to 12 hours after the laughter in some cases, in L. S. Berk, D. L. Felton, S. A. Tan, B. B. Bittman, and J. Westengard, 'Modulation of neuroimmune parameters during the eustress of mirthful Laughter,' *Alternative Therapies*, 2001, 7(2), 62-76.

3. For effects of laughter on some hormone levels see L. S. Berk, S. A. Tan, W. F. Fry, B. J. Napier, J. W. Lee, R. W. Hubbard, J. E. Lewis, and W. C. Eby, 'Neuroendocrine and stress hormone changes during mirthful laughter,' *The American Journal of the Medical Sciences*, 1989, 298(6), 390-396.

4. For the story of Norman Cousins and his laughter-aided recovery from a serious illness see Norman Cousins, 'Anatomy of an illness,' *New England J. Medicine*, 1976, 295, 1458-1463. Norman discovered that 10 minutes of genuine belly laughter had an anaesthetic effect and allowed him about 2 hours pain free sleep.

For physiological effects of Meditation see Paramahansa Yogananda, *Autobiography of a Yogi*, (Self-Realization Fellowship, Los Angeles, Thirteenth Ed., 1998) and for physiological effects and examples of meditation techniques see book by Dharma Singh Khalsa MD and Cameron Stauth, *Meditation as Medicine*, (Pocket Books, New York, 2001).

Botox is a snake venom that is used in cosmetic procedures to temporarily paralyse some of the muscles on the forehead. Through this paralysis it removes the appearance of wrinkles on the forehead and around the eyes by completely relaxing the muscles.

For the story of the man who visualised a healthy liver see the book by Carolyn Miller Ph.D., *Creating Miracles* (H. J. Kramer Inc, CA, 1995).

For creative visualisation techniques see Shakti Gawain, *Creative Visualisation*, (Natoraj Publishing, CA, 1995), as well as Ed Bernd and Ian Pollock, *Silva Method*, (The Silva Method Publishing, Glasgow, 2001).

For the connection between suppressed negative emotion and cancer see:

1. For summary of 18 individual scientific studies see James Gross, 'Emotional expression in cancer onset and progression,' *Soc. Sci. Med.*, 1989, 28(12), 1239-1248.

2. For an early published correlation between personality type and the progression of cancer see E. Blumberg, P. West, and F. Ellis, 'A possible relationship between psychological factors and human cancer,' *Psychosom. Res.*, 1954, 16, 27-86.

3. To see the relationship between Type C personality and tumour thickness see L. Temoshok, B. W. Heller, R. W. Sagebiel, M. S. Blois, D. M. Sweet, R. J. Di Clemente, and

M. L. Gold, 'The relationship of psychosocial factors to prognostic indicators in cutaneous malignant melanoma,' *J. Psychosom. Res.*, 1985, 29, 139-154.

For the positive effects of release of suppressed negative emotion on cancer see:

1. J. W. Pennebaker, J. K. Kiecolt-Glaser, and R. Glaser, 'Disclosure of traumas and immune function: Health implications for psychotherapy,' *J. Consult. Clin. Psychol.*, 1988, 56, 239-245.

2. D. Spiegel, J. Bloom, H. C. Kramer, et al, 'Effect of psychological treatment on survival of patients with metastatic breast cancer,' *Lancet*, 1989, 2, 888-891.

For the relationship between coming 'out of the closet' and HIV and AIDS progression see S. W. Cole, M. E. Kemeny, S. E Taylor, B. R. Visscher, and J. L. Fahey, 'Accelerated course of human immunodeficiency virus infection in gay men who conceal their homosexual identity,' *Psychosom. Med.*, 1996, 58, 219-231.

For the story of Brandon Bays and her recovery from a basketball sized tumour see Brandon Bays, *The Journey*, (HarperCollins, 1999).

Chapter 2 - The Power of Faith

For general examples and description of the placebo effect see Herbert Benson, *Timeless Healing - The Power and Biology of Belief*, (Simon & Schuster, London, 1996).

For specific examples of the placebo effect see:

1. For the example of the placebo effect and morning sickness see S. Wolff, 'Effects of suggestion and conditioning on the action of chemical agents in human subjects: The pharmacology of placebos,' *Journal of Clinical Investigation*, 1950, 29, 100-109.

2. For the example of placebo effect and asthma see C. Butler and A. Steptoe, 'Placebo responses: An experimental study of psychophysiological processes in asthmatic volunteers,' *British Journal of Clinical Psychology*, 1986, 25, 173-183.

3. For the effect of colour on the placebo effect see G. S. Kienle and H. Kiene, 'Placebo effects from packaging, formulation, colour, and size of the placebo,' in 'Placebo effect and placebo concept: A critical methodological and conceptual analysis of reports on the magnitude of the placebo effect,' *Alternative Therapies*, 1996, 2, 39-54, cited in L. Dossey, *Healing Beyond the Body*, (Time Warner, London, 2001).

For history of psychoneuroimmunology, the discovery of the opiate receptor, and how neuropeptides and their receptors work see Candace. B. Pert Ph.D., *Molecules of Emotion*, (Touchstone, New York, 1997).

For summary papers on psychoneuroimmunology and the role of neuropeptides see:

1.   C. B. Pert, H. E. Dreher, and M. D. Ruff, 'The psychosomatic network: Foundations of mind-body medicine,' *Alternative Therapies*, 1998, 4(4), 30-41.

2.   C. B. Pert, M. R. Ruff, R. J. Weber, and M. Herkenham, 'Neuropeptides and their receptors: A psychosomatic network,' *J. Immunol.*, 1985, 35(2), 820s-826s.

For the role of neuropeptides with emotional centres in the brain, and in the immune system, see:

1.   M. E. Ruff, V. Schiffman, V. Terranova, and C. B. Pert, 'Neuropeptides are chemoattractants for human tumour cells and monocytes: A possible mechanism for metastasis,' *Clin. Immunol. Immunopathol.*, 1985, 37, 387-396.

2.   M. R. Ruff, S. M. Wahl, S. Mergenhagen, and C. B. Pert, 'Opiate receptor-mediated chemotaxis of human monocytes,' *Neuropeptides*, 1985, 5, 363.

For Bi-directional communication between emotions and immune system see D. J. Carr and J. E. Blalock, 'Neuropeptide hormones and receptors common to the immune and neuroendocrine systems: Bi-directional pathway of intersystem communication,' In R. Ader, D. L. Felten, and N. Cohen, Eds, *Psychoneuroimmunology II*, (Academic Press, New York, 1991).

For the role of opioids in the placebo effect see:

1.   J. D. Levine, N. C. Gordon, and H. L. Fields, 'The Mechanism of placebo analgesia,' *Lancet*, 1978, 654-657.

2.   F. Benedetti, M. Amanzio, and G. Maggi, 'Potentiation of placebo analgesia by proglumide,' *Lancet*, 1995, 346, 1231.

3.   G. ter Riet, A. J. M. de Craen, A. de Boer, and A. G. H. Kessels, "Is placebo analgesia mediated by endogenous opioids? A systematic review,' *Pain*, 1998, 76, 273-275.

4.   F. Benedetti, A. Pollo, L. Lopiano, M. Lanotte, S. Vighetti, and I. Rainero, 'Conscious expectation and unconscious conditioning in analgesic, motor, and hormonal placebo/nocebo responses,' *J. Neuroscience*, 2003, 23(10), 4315-4323.

5.   A. Pollo, S. Vighetti, I. Rainero, and F. Benedetti, 'Placebo analgesia and the heart,' *Pain*, 2003, 102, 125-133.

For Brain imaging scans of opioid versus placebo analgesia see P. Petrovic, E. Kalso, K. M. Petersson, and M. Ingvar, 'Placebo and opioid analgesia – Imaging a shared neuronal network,' *Science*, 2002, 295, 1737-1740.

For role of neuropeptides as informational substances see F. D. Schmitt, 'Molecular regulation of brain function: A new view,' *Neuroscience*, 1984, 13, 991.

For neuropeptide approaches to cancer and AIDS see Candace. B. Pert Ph.D., *Molecules of Emotion*, (Touchstone, New York, 1997).

Chapter 3 - DNA

For discovery of the double helix structure of DNA see J. Watson and F. Crick, 'A structure for deoxyribose nucleic acid,' *Nature*, 1953, 171, 737.

For the role played by Rosalind Franklin in the discovery of the structure of DNA see Brenda Maddox, 'The double helix and the 'Wronged Heroine',' *Nature*, 2003, 421, 407-408.

For the role of Interleukin-2 in recovery from cancer see:
1. S. Rosenberg and J. Barry, *The Transformed Cell: Unlocking the Mysteries of Cancer*, (Putnam/Chapmans, New York, 1992).
2. J. Newman, *I Have Seen Cancers Disappear*, (Interview with Steven Rosenberg), *Discover*, 2001, 22, 44-51.

For the effect of loving maternal touch on gene expression in rat pups see S. Wang, J. Bartolome, and S. Schanberg, 'Neonatal deprivation of maternal touch may suppress ornithine decarboxylase via downregulation of the protooncogenes c-myc and max,' *J. Neuroscience*, 1996, 16(2), 836-842. Also summarised in E. L. Rossi, 'Psychosocial Genomics: Gene expression, neurogenesis, and human experience in mind-body medicine,' *Advances*, 2002, 18(2), 22-30.

For a summary of research in psychosocial genomics see the book by Ernest L. Rossi, *The Psychobiology of Gene Expression: Neuroscience and Neurogenesis in Hypnosis and the Healing Arts,* (Norton, NY, 2002).

See also:

1. Ernest Rossi, 'Stress-Induced Alternative Gene Splicing in Mind-Body Medicine,' *Advances,* 2004, 20(2), 12-19
2. Ernest Rossi, 'Gene Expression, Neurogenesis, and Healing: Psychosocial Genomics of Therapeutic Hypnosis,' *American Journal of Clinical Hypnosis,* 2003, 45(3), 197-216

For information about Nature Vs Nurture, including examples of relative roles of genes and the environment in human growth and development see Matt Ridley, *Nature Via Nurture: Genes, Experience, and What Makes us Human,* (Harper Perennial, London, 2004) and Tim Spector, *Your Genes Unzipped: How your Genetic Inheritance Shapes your Life,* (Robson Books, London, 2003). These books were also the source of the figures of the differences in genes between humans and other species.

For some of Eric Kandel's work see, Eric R. Kandel, M.D., 'A New Intellectual Framework for Psychiatry,' *Americal Journal of Psychiatry,* 1998, 155(4), 457-469

For general information about the role of emotional environment in the growth of the prefrontal lobes in infants and children see Joseph Chilton Pearce, *The Biology of Transcendence,* (Park Street Press, Rochester, Vermont, 2002).

For a description of psychosocial dwarfism or nonorganic failure-to-thrive see L. Gardner, 'Deprivation Dwarfism,' *Scientific American*, 1972, 227(1), 76-82.

For studies on the effect of emotional deprivation and lack of touch on growth hormone levels see:
1. G. Powell, N. Hopwood, and E. Baratt, 'Growth hormone studies before and during catch-up growth in a child with emotional deprivation and short stature,' *J. Clin. Endocrinol. Metab.*, 1973, 37(5), 674-679.
2. G. Powell, J. Brasel, and J. Hansen, 'Emotional deprivation and growth retardation simulating idiopathic hypopituitarism: I. Clinical evaluation of the syndrome,' *New England J. Medicine.*, 1967, 276(23), 1271-1278.

For information about ADHD see Thom Hartmann, *Attention Deficit Disorder: A Different Perception*, (Underwood Books, 1997).

Although 99.9% of our genes are known to be the same there exists at least 3 million natural subtle variations in the individual genes. These are known as single nucleotide polymorphisms (SNP's) and it is believed that they give rise to some of our individuality.

Chapter 4 – The Power of Intention
For a summary of Bernard Grad's Research on healing see:
1. Bernard R. Grad, 'Some biological effects of laying-on of hands: A review of experiments with animals and plants,'

Journal of the American Society for Psychical Research, 1965, 59, 95-127.

2.   Bernard R. Grad, 'The laying on of hands: Implications for psychotherapy, gentling and placebo effect,' *Journal of the American Society for Psychical Research*, 1967, 61, 286-305.

For the effects of healing touch on enzymes see:

1.   J. Smith, 'The influence on enzyme growth by the 'Laying on of Hands,' *The dimensions of healing: A symposium*, Los Altos, CA: The Academy of Parapsychology and Medicine, 1972.

2.   Toni Bunnell, 'The effect of 'healing with intent' on pepsin enzyme activity,' *J. Sci. Explor.*, 1999, 13(2), 139-148.

For effects on E-coli see C. B. Nash, 'Test of psychokinetic control of bacterial mutation,' *J. Am. Soc. Psychical Res.*, 1984, 78(2), 145-152.

For description of Paramahansa Yogananda's discussions with Luther Burbank see Paramahansa Yogananda, *Autobiography of a Yogi*, (Self Realization Fellowship, Los Angeles, CA, Thirteenth Ed. 1998).

For general understanding and scientific studies on acupuncture see Richard Gerber MD, *Vibrational Medicine for the 21st Century*, (Piatkus, London, 2000).

For a summary of Qigong research see K. M. Sancier, 'Medical applications of Qigong,' *Alternative Therapies*, 1996, 2(1), 40-46.

General Healing by touch and intention references can be found in Daniel J. Benor, *Healing Research, Volume I: Spiritual Healing: Scientific Validation Of A Healing Revolution*, (Vision Publications, Southfield, MI, 2001).

Chapter 5 - Good Vibrations

For a summary of research, on the effects of healing touch and intention on water, by William Tiller and others see William A. Tiller Ph.D., *Science and Human Transformation: Subtle Energies, Intentionality, and Consciousness*, (Pavior, CA, 1997).

Dr Glen Rein's research on the effects of human intention on DNA was gained in a personal discussion with him. Some of his work is summarised in William Tiller's book listed above.

For general information about homeopathy, Bach flower remedies, and vibrational medicine see Richard Gerber MD, *Vibrational Medicine for the 21st Century*, (Piatkus, London, 2000).

For information about vibrational solutions of a rock called *Aulterra* see work by Kim Dandurand. Kim discovered that a highly paramagnetic rock substance called *Aulterra*, and its vibrational essence produced by succussion in water, had healing properties. General analysis showed this to be correct and showed that the rock energised water and food substances that it came into contact with, or was held close to. Kirlian photographs also showed a powerful energy field emanating from the rock and from food supplements that it was held close to. I have personally tested Aulterra and found that holding it close to water, and then using that water on cress seeds, caused an increase in their rate of growth in a seven day experiment. For general information about Aulterra and some of the scientific studies see www.aulterra.com.

For information on paramagnetism and its affects on biology and plants see Philip S. Callahan Ph.D., *Paramagnetism*, (Acres USA, Austin, TX, 1995).

For Jacques Benveniste's scientific paper showing highly dilute effects of the anti-IgE antibody see E. Davenas, F. Beauvais, J. Amara, M. Oberbaum, B. Robinzon, A. Miadonna, A. Tedeschi, B. Poweranz, P. Fortner, P. Belon, J. Sainte-Laudy, B. Poitevin, and J. Benveniste, 'Human basophil degranulation triggered by very dilute antiserum against IgE, ' *Nature*, 1988, 333, 816-818.

For further scientific evidence of the power of homeopathy see David Reilly, 'Is evidence for homeopathy reproducible?' *Lancet*, 1994, 344, 1601-1606.

For some Digital Biology (Electromagnetic Molecular Signalling - EMS) research by Professor Jacques Benveniste see:
1. J. Benveniste, B. Arnoux, and L. Hadji, 'Highly dilute antigen increases coronary flow of isolated heart from immunized guinea-pigs,' *FASEB Journal*, 1992, 6, A1610.

2. J. Benveniste, J. Aissa, and D. Guillonet, 'Digital Biology: Specificity of the digitised molecular signal,' *FASEB Journal*, 1998, 12, A412 (2392).

3. J. Benveniste, P. Jurgens, and J, Aissa, 'Digital recording/transmission of the cholinergic signal,' *FASEB Journal*, 1996, 10: A1479.

4. Y. Thomas, M. Schiff, M. H. Litime, L. Belkadi, and J. Benveniste, 'Direct transmission to cells of a molecular signal (phorbol myristate acetate, PMA) via an electronic device,' *FASEB Journal*, 1995, 9, A227.

5. J. Aissa, M. H. Litime, E. Attias, and J. Benveniste, 'Molecular signalling at high dilution or by means of electronic circuitry,' *Journal of Immunology*, 1993, 150, 146A (830).

6. J. Benveniste, L. Kahhak, and D. Guillonet, 'Specific remote detection of bacteria using an electromagnetic / digital procedure,' *FASEB Journal*, 1999, 13, A852(645.22).

7. For information on digital biology and a full list of Professor Benveniste's papers see www.digibio.com.

For sending a digitised signal along a telephone line see J. Benveniste, P. Jurges, W. Hsuch, and J. Aissa, 'Transatlantic transfer of digitised antigen by telephone link,' *J. Allergy and Clinical Immunology*, 1997, 99(1) part 2, S:175 (705).

For a summary of some of Jacques Benveniste's digital biology work see Lynn McTaggart, *The Field*, (Harper Collins, London, 2001).

For the effect of some pieces of music on the immune system see R. McCraty, M. Atkinson, G. Rein, and A. Watkins, 'Music enhances the effect of positive emotional states on salivary Immunoglobulin A,' *Stress Medicine*, 1996, 12, 167-175.

For effects of drumming on the immune system see B. B. Bittman, L. S. Berk, D. L. Felten, J. Westengard, C. Simonton, J. Pappas, and M. Ninehouser, 'Composite effects of group drumming music therapy on modulation of neuroendocrine-immune parameters in normal subjects,' *Alternative Therapies*, 2001, 7(1), 38-47.

For information about the Japa meditation see Wayne Dyer, *Getting In The Gap*, (Hay House, CA, 2003).

For some effects of sound on cancer cells see, www.tama-do.com

For information about use of sound in healing see www.soundintentions.com

Effects of words on growth of cress seeds

Below is a summary list of my own research into the effects of words on the height of cress sprouts over the course of 7 days. Each word was written on a label and stuck onto a cup. Water was then added to the cup and immediately used to water six pots of 50 seeds. Each measurement below represents the average seed height of 50 sprouts. The mean figures are therefore an average for 300 seeds.

	Love (height of sprouts in mm)	**Fear** (height of sprouts in mm)	**Happy** (height of sprouts in mm)	**Sad** (height of sprouts in mm)	**Control** (height of sprouts in mm)
Mean	45.39	42.43	46.06	40.14	43.34

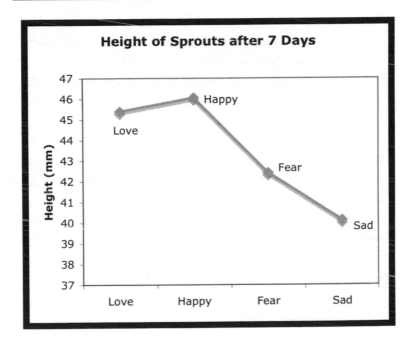

For photographs of the effects of words, emotions, and music on water crystals see Masaru Emoto, *Messages from Water*, (Hado, 1999) and *The Hidden Messages in Water*, (Beyond Worlds, 2004).

Chapter 6 - Distant Healing and Prayer

For the effect of mental activation and calming of targets see D. J. Radin, R. K. Taylor, and W. G. Braud, 'Remote mental influence of human electrodermal activity: A preliminary replication,' *Proceedings of The Parapsychological Association 36th Annual Conference*, 1993, p12-13.

For a summary of research on distant healing see:

1. Elisabeth Targ, 'Evaluating distant healing: A Research Review,' *Alternative Therapies*, 1997, 3(6), 74-78.
2. Marilyn Schlitz and William Braud, 'Distant intentionality and healing: Assessing the evidence,' *Alternative Therapies*, 1997, 3(6), 62-73.

For a study of the effect of distant intention on hypertension see R. N. Miller, 'Study on the effectiveness of remote mental healing,' *Med. Hypoth.*, 1982, 8, 481-490.

For study of distant effects on blood see:

1. William Braud, 'Distant mental influence of rate of hemolysis,' *Research in Parapsychology*, 1989.
2. William Braud, 'Distant mental influence on rate of hemolysis of human red blood cells,' *J. Am Soc. Psychical Res.*, 1990, 84, 1-24.

For distant intentional effects on fungus see:

1. J. Barry, 'General and comparative study of the psychokinetic effect on a fungus culture,' *J. Parapsychology*, 1968, 32(4), 237-243.

2. W. Tedder and M. Monty, 'Exploration of long distance PK: A conceptual replication of the influence on a biological system,' in W. G. Roll et al, Eds, *Research in Parapsychology*, 1980, 90-93.

Information about increase in growth rate of rye grass at 500km can be found on an audio tape set by Richard Gerber MD, *Exploring Vibrational Medicine*, (Sounds True, Boulder, CO, 1997).

For a study of distant influence on mental concentration see W. Braud, D. Shafer, K. McNeill, and V. Guerra, 'Attention focusing facilitated remote mental interaction,' *Proceedings of The Parapsychological Association 36th Annual Conference*, 1993, p1-11

Prayer

For effects of prayer on recovery from heart operations see:

1. Randolph C. Byrd, 'Positive therapeutic effects of intercessory prayer in a coronary care unit population,' *Southern Medical Journal*, 1988, 81, 826-829.

2. M. W. Krucoff, S. W. Crater, C. L. Green, A. C. Maas, J. E. Seskevich, J. D. Lane, K. a. Loeffler, K. Morris, T. M. Bashore, H. G. Koenig, 'Integrative noetic therapies as adjuncts to precutaneous intervention during unstable coronary syndromes: Monitoring and actualisation of

noetic training (MANTRA) feasibility pilot,' *American Heart Journal*, 2001, 142, 760-797.

For experiments where people praying received as much benefit as the people they prayed for see S. O'Laoire, 'An experimental study of the effects of distant, intercessory prayer on self-esteem, anxiety, and depression,' *Alternative Therapies*, 1997, 3(6), 38-53.

For information on Tibetan praying techniques and prayer information from the Dead Sea Scrolls see Gregg Braden, The Isaiah Effect, (Harmony Books, New York, 2000).

Chapter 7 - The Nature of Reality

For information on Quantum Theory and the Connectedness of things see:

1. Gary Zukav, *The Dancing Wu Li Masters*, (Rider, London, 1979).

2. John Gribbin, *In Search of Scroedinger's Cat*, (Black Swan, London, 1984).

3. Brian D. Josephson and Fotini Pallikari-Viras, 'Biological utilization of quantum nonlocality,' *Foundations of Physics*, 1991, 21(2), 197-207.

4. Euan J. Squires, 'Quantum theory and the relation between the conscious mind and the physical world,' *Synthese*, 1993, 97, 109-123.

5. J. S. Bell, 'On the Einstein-Podolsky-Rosen paradox,' *Physics*, 1964, 1, 195-200.

6.   A. Einstein, B. Podolsky, and N. Rosen, 'Can quantum-
     mechanical description of physical reality be considered
     complete?,' *Phys. Rev.*, 1935, 47, 777-780.

There are obvious parallels between my description of condensing consciousness and the collapse of the wavefunction in theoretical quantum physics, coupled with Bell's Theorem, and the modern belief that consciousness is the basic building block of reality – that being aware of something changes it. This is intended. I have made my own interpretations of the theories too which led to the simplistic description that I present. Due to the complex nature of the subject I chose a visibly simple method of describing reality that is easily understood by most people.

For a metaphysical view see Jane Roberts, *The Nature of Personal Reality (A Seth book)*, (Amber Allen, San Rafael, CA, 1994).

For information about chaordic businesses and chaordic management see Dee Hock, *Birth of the Chaordic Age*, (Berret-Koehler, San Francisco, 1999).

Chapter 8 - Experiments in Connectedness

For a good summary of research using random event generators and for work on ESP see Dean I. Radin, *The Conscious Universe*, (HarperCollins, New York, 1997).

For information on the charity Spirit Aid see, www.spiritaid.org.uk. The original Spirit Aid event was titled

'World Energy Day' and was intended for October 2001. As more people joined the organising team the name changed and the time was re-scheduled for July 2002 and was planned to take place in a football stadium. However funding challenges led to its taking the form of a 9-day, 24-event festival of peace featuring scaled down elements of the originally planned event. The festival also included: a peace walk up a Scottish Mountain (Ben Lomond), a conference, a concert, a peace procession through the city, talks, workshops, a picnic for peace, meditations, and the children of Glasgow made 50 metres of James Twyman's 'Children's Cloth of Many Colours' where they each wrote a peace message on a small piece of cloth that was then sewn onto the main cloth.

For information about James Twyman see www.emissaryoflight.com
For information about Gregg Braden see www.greggbraden.net
For information about Doreen Virtue see www.angeltherapy.com

For a summary of ESP experiments between 1964 and 1993 see Julie Milton, 'Ordinary state ESP meta analysis,' in *Proceedings of The Parapsychological Association 36th Annual Conference*, M. J. Schlitz, Ed., 1993.

For effect of hypnosis on ESP ability see R. G. Stanford and A.G. Stein, 'A meta-analysis of ESP studies contrasting hypnosis and a comparison condition,' *Journal of Parapsychology*, 1994, 58(3), 235-270.

For information that ESP is affected by beliefs, and which also shows the effect of hypnosis, see L. Casler, 'The improvement of clairvoyant scores by means of hypnotic suggestion,' *Journal of Parapsychology*, 1962, 26, 77-87. The paper suggests that people block their ESP and clairvoyant abilities because of 1) Fears of social ridicule, 2) Early learning that this sort of stuff is not possible, and 3) they may not be prepared to alter their view of themselves or the universe that a belief in ESP might cause them to do. If these beliefs are changed to ones that accept ESP and clairvoyancy then both ESP and clairvoyancy become easier. I also discovered this is my personal unpublished experiments with ESP, and with conscious influence of random event generators, both in 1993. The more I believed that I could do it, the better were my results.

For Wayne Dyer's book see Wayne Dyer, *You'll See It When You Believe It*, (HarperCollins, 1989).

For a summary analysis of sheep-goat experiments see Tony Lawrence, 'Gathering in the sheep and goats: A meta analysis of forced choice sheep-goat ESP studies, 1947-1993,' *Proceedings of The Parapsychological Association 36th Annual Conference*, M. J. Schlitz, Ed., 1993, 75-86.

Chapter 9 - Who Am I?
For a great book discussing the nature of our being see Eckhart Tolle, *The Power of Now*, (Hodder and Stoughton, London, 1999).

Chapter 10 - Love, Fear, and Biology

The references for some of this chapter are listed in other chapters because most of the research quoted is a summary of pieces quoted in previous chapters. For ease I have listed some of the specific sources here again.

For the effect of love on atherosclerosis in rabbits see R. M. Nerem, M. J. Levesque, and J. F. Cornhill, 'Social environment as a factor in diet-induced atherosclerosis,' *Science*, 1980, 208, 1475-1476.

For the effects of a loving environment on the growth of the prefrontal lobes in the brains of infants and children see Joseph Chilton Pearce, *The Biology of Transcendence*, (Park Street Press, Rochester, Vermont, 2002).

The example of the cacti giving up their thorns when they were tenderly spoken to can be found in the book, *Autobiography of a Yogi*, by Paramahansa Yogananda, (Self Realization Fellowship, Los Angeles, CA, Thirteenth Ed. 1998) which is dedicated to the memory of Luther Burbank.

For studies on the effects of appreciation, care, and compassion as well as anger and frustration on the heart and immune system see:
1. R. McCraty, M. Atkinson, W. A. Tiller, G. Rein, and A. D. Watkins, 'The effects of emotions on short-term power spectrum analysis of heart rate variability, *Am. Journal of Cardiology*, 1995, 76, 1089-1093.

2.   G. Rein, M. Atkinson, and R. McCraty, 'The physiological and psychological effects of compassion and anger, *J. Advancement in Med.*, 1995, 8(2), 87-105.

For a summary of the effects of maternal touch on gene expression see Ernest. L. Rossi, 'Psychosocial Genomics: Gene expression, neurogenesis, and human experience in mind-body medicine,' *Advances*, 2002, 18(2), Winter, 22-30.

For effects of love and intention on DNA see:
1.   G. Rein and R. McCraty, 'Structural changes in water and DNA associated with new physiologically measurable states,' *Proc. Society for Scientific Exploration Conf.*, Austin, TX, June 1994.
2.   G. Rein and R. McCraty, 'Local and non-local effects of coherent heart frequencies on conformational changes of DNA,' *Proc. Joint USPA/IAPR Psychotronics Conf.*, Milwaukee, 1993.
3.   The above references also cited and summarised in William A. Tiller, *Science and Human Transformation: Subtle Energies, Intentionality, and Consciousness*, (Pavior, CA, 1997).

Chapter 11 - Mass Reality

For a metaphysical view on the mass creation of reality see Jane Roberts, *The Individual And The Nature Of Mass Events (A Seth book)*, (Amber-Allen, San Rafael, CA, 1995).

For information on Hundredth Monkey and similar experiments see Thom Hartmann, *The Prophet's Way*, (Hodder and Stoughton, London, 2002).

Chapter 12 - DNA – II

Information about cyclic spurts of growth of the brain can be found in Joseph Chilton Pearce, *The Biology of Transcendence*, (Park Street Press, Rochester, Vermont, 2002).

For information about sounds and harmonics see www.soundintentions.com

On the Higher Self choosing the genes. There is no contradiction with the laws of genetics and inheritance. I believe that each Higher Self chooses particular genes within the framework of what is possible within such laws. Perhaps the randomness in the process of inheriting genes is not so random!

For information about man-made damage to rainforests and to biodiversity see Thom Hartmann, *The Last Hours of Ancient Sunlight*, (Three Rivers Press, New York, 1999) and the section 'Earth Changes' in the Appendix of *The Prophet's Way*, (Hodder and Stoughton, London, 2002).

Chapters 14 – Three Simple Rules

There are no cited references for chapters 13 & 14, however to read teachings and stories of love and kindness I would recommend the works of Gary Zukav and those of Wayne Dyer Ph.D., as well as the *Chicken Soup* series, founded by Jack Canfield and Mark Victor Hansen, and the *Conversations with God* books by Neal Donald Walsch.

For information on talks or workshops given by
Dr David R. Hamilton or to book him for a
speaking event e-mail:

davidhamilton1970@yahoo.co.uk

Notes

Notes

Notes

Notes

Notes

Notes